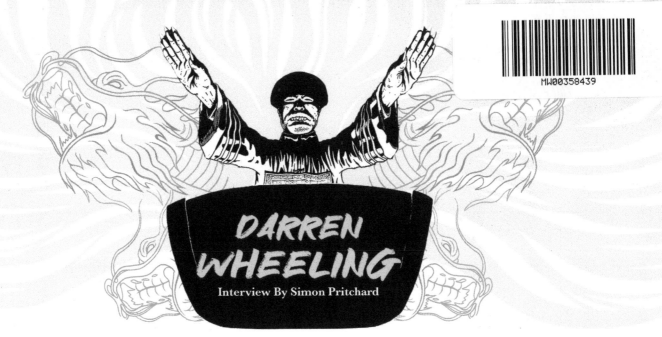

DARREN WHEELING

Interview By Simon Pritchard

Darren was raised just outside of Washington DC, USA. A budding artist since he was young, he grew up creating his own comics and producing animation.

He may be best known to HK movie fans for his cover artwork for Eureka Entertainment (as well as Arrow, Nova Media and Koch Films), or perhaps his contributions to Oriental Cinema and Video Magazine back in the day.

But Darren has also been working behind the scenes for several Blu-Ray houses providing rare footage; photos, subtitles, audio tracks, and more.

Professionally, Darren has run his own graphic design firm since 1991 creating corporate branding, product packaging, storyboarding, web design, and more. And a few Hong Kong movie covers too.

SP: What were the first comic books you got into?

DW: I have two older brothers so I got handed down their collection of the 1960s-1970s Marvel and DC comics but what probably influenced me more was the stack of MAD magazines they gave me. I especially loved the exaggerated cartoons of Don Martin and Basil Wolverton. And the intricate design of the SPY vs. SPY gags by Antonio Prohais.

SP: Whilst a lot of kids like to draw, at what point did you realise that you had a real talent for it?

DW: Well, all I ever wanted to be was a visual artist. I knew from around age

five. But ART is a pretty wide field. What "art" I was exposed to as a kid was mostly comics and animation, so naturally, my interest developed in that direction from an early age. I was in advanced placement art classes and won awards and art scholarships. But the shift to digital art came after my formal education, so that's been a personal learning experience

adapting to the changing times. The tools I use every day did not exist when I was in college, but the fundamentals I learned can still be applied.

SP: What artists and genres have inspired you throughout your life?

DW: Inspiration can come from just about anywhere, but I really admire the work of Dave McKean, Chris Ware, Frank Frazetta, Vaughan Oliver, Bob Peak and Syd Mead (among others).

SP: How did you get into Asian cinema and Hong Kong films?

DW: I discovered HK film by catching PEKING OPERA BLUES at an art house theatre in 1988. I was blown away by the colourful pageantry. It had everything from political intrigue, farce-style comedy, Chinese cultural history, high-flying action, and three of the most beautiful women as leads. What's NOT to like? I felt compelled to discover more films like this, as well as learn more about Chinese cultural history. I was never the same after that.

I quickly discovered a Chinese theatre that showed nothing but HK double features for $6 USD. The films changed every week so it became my Sunday night ritual. My "house of worship". Despite my dedicated attendance, they closed in June 1989. (Not too surprising as often I was nearly the only one inside, save for a couple of Asian teens in the back row and a homeless

person in the corner who'd come inside to get dry.)

Soon after I joined nearly 30 video clubs just to rent (hire, I think the Brits say) one or two of the HK titles in their foreign film section. Later I discovered three local Chinese video rental stores. Woo hoo! Now we're talking!

SP: You have a treasure trove of Asian cinema, many of which people thought was lost in the mists of time. How did you manage to build such a collection?

DW: Since I was spending so much time at one particular Chinese video store I ended up developing a friendship with the owner. We'd go see HK Canto Pop concerts (Andy Lau, Anita Mui, Sally Yeh, and Leon Lai, etc.) and I offered to help rearrange the stock as they did not have the VHS tapes organized by genre. Being an artist, and taking Mandarin classes at night, I could make bilingual shelf labels. Eventually, this led to a marriage that's still going strong. (Honestly, it was LOVE, the free HK movies were just a bonus!)

But by 1996 the HK industry was in major decline and we shuttered the store. Luckily I kept hundreds of my fave VHS tapes when we closed up, as many of these were the rarer longer Taiwanese cuts that have since been hard to find on DVD. (Did you know the Taiwanese version of TWIN DRAGONS has 11 extra frames, more than the HK version, of Jackie getting out of the hot tub? Yeah, I counted.)

I was by this time a serious collector of HK movie "stuff". Books, posters, lobbies, Laser Discs, whatever. I'd make trips to HK and buy suitcases there just to fill up and ship home. (How many DVDs in their cases fit inside the largest hard suitcase you can check on a plane? Answer: Around 81!)

SP: Firstly, thank you on behalf of every Fu fan; how did your collection make it onto the latest boutique special edition discs?

DW: A few years ago, even though I'm not interested in social media, word got out online about my collection, and some fans making customs have reached out to me for help. "Hey, do you mind ripping your Laser Disc so I can use the original mono soundtrack?" "Hey, do you have such and such?" Then, when the boutique labels

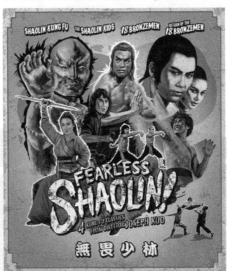

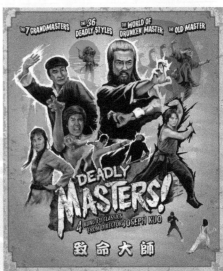

finally stepped up to fill the void I was asked to do the same for them. In many cases, the fans know more about these old films than the current license holders.

These recent releases are truly a global effort from dedicated people in various countries all chipping in. Truly a labour of love. I provide rare photos, trailers,

to do the packaging design. So I still help out behind the scenes, but I do the covers too when offered the opportunity. It's that magical, and often elusive, combination of passion and profession.

SP: It seems like Arrow Video, Eureka Entertainment, and 88 Films work in harmony in regard to the special features and region coding of their discs. Whilst it's awesome for fans, this is pretty unheard of for rival companies, how does this all work?

DW: The way I see it, a high tide raises all boats. A healthy home video market is good for everyone. So yes, there's a friendly competition, but each distributor purchases the rights for different markets and the licensee provides as much content as they can. It's up to the boutiques to supplement that with their own unique material to make their version stand out. As a fan, I love that they care enough to compete to make the best home video version. I also enjoy seeing other artists' designs for covers. Sadly, many US distributors put in the minimal effort because there is no Region A alternative. No competition. It's the fans who suffer. Only Criterion seems to care about the US market for HK classics.

SP: You have drawn the majority of the covers for the boutique special edition discs, what are your favourite ones you have done?

DW: Well I guess there's always a backstory to each cover. My father, whom I was caring for, passed away while I was working on KING BOXER (for Arrow) and PROPHECY (for Eureka) so I remember those moments. I don't have a specific favourite. What I try to do is create the most suitable style of art I can for each title. I don't want to have a signature style that I force into every project. It's an uphill but worthwhile struggle to push myself into different visual directions while staying inside the box of what fans want.

SP: Are there any films that have not had the special edition treatment that you would love to draw for and see released?

DW: Of course PEKING OPERA BLUES, SHANGHAI BLUES, FULL

references for colour grading, etc. Whatever they ask me for. If I have it, I'm happy to share it to help restore these classics. My wife and I provided English

subs for the "Happy Happy Gala Gala" song in CITY HUNTER as Fortune Star provided no translation. After doing that for a while someone asked if I would like

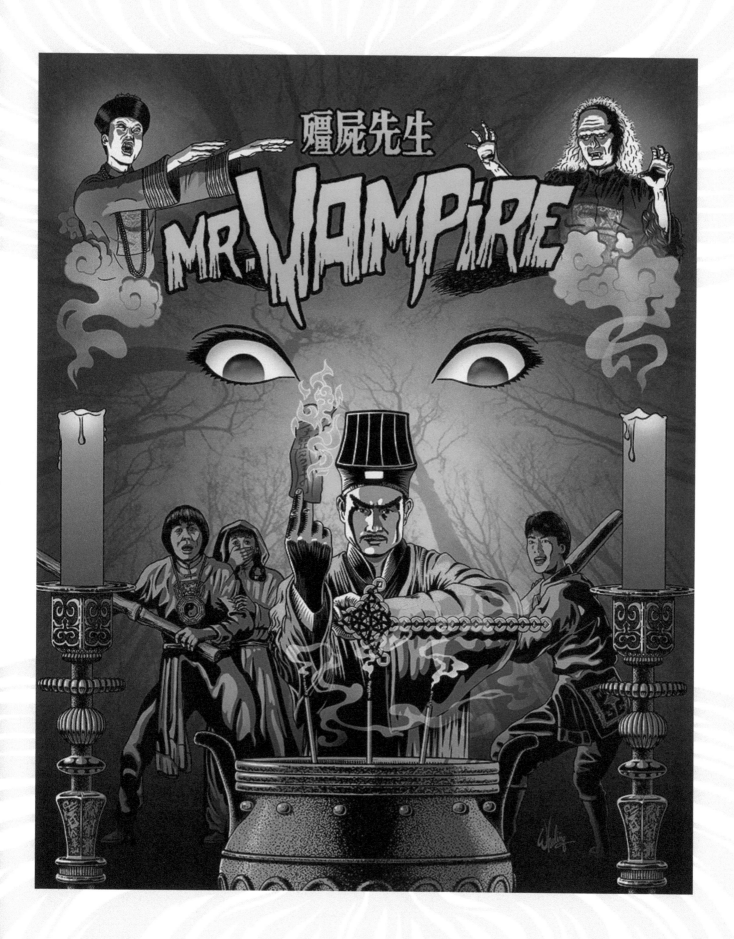

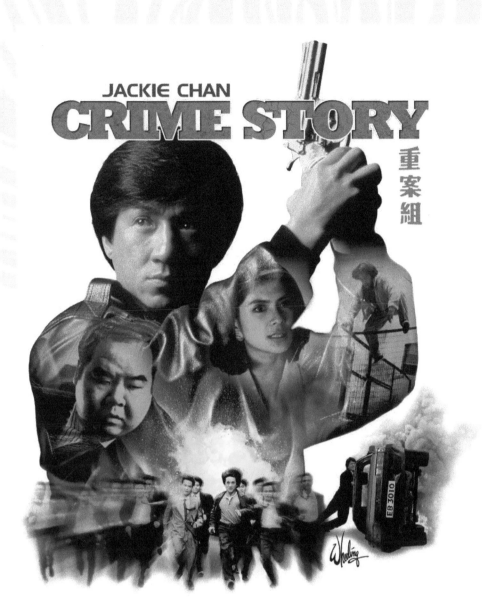

CONTACT, ONCE A THIEF, I LOVE MARIA (ROBOFORCE), and the ANGEL Series. I'd love to see a label do some double or triple-feature sets of lesser-known titles. Like a HK THRILLER set of WEB OF DECEPTION + FATAL LOVE + HER VENGEANCE or a Chow Yun-fat set of AN AUTUMN'S TALE + ALL ABOUT AH-LONG + NOW YOU SEE LOVE, NOW YOU DON'T. It does get a bit tiring when the same Jackie Chan movies get released 10 times and these other really good films never get exposure outside of SouthEast Asia. But I understand the financial reasoning behind it.

SP: I think your covers stand out not only for the detail but also for the use of strong background colours. The orange, red and yellow mix or

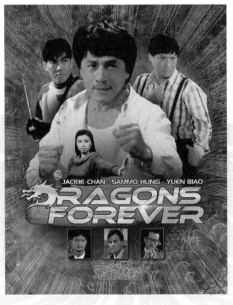

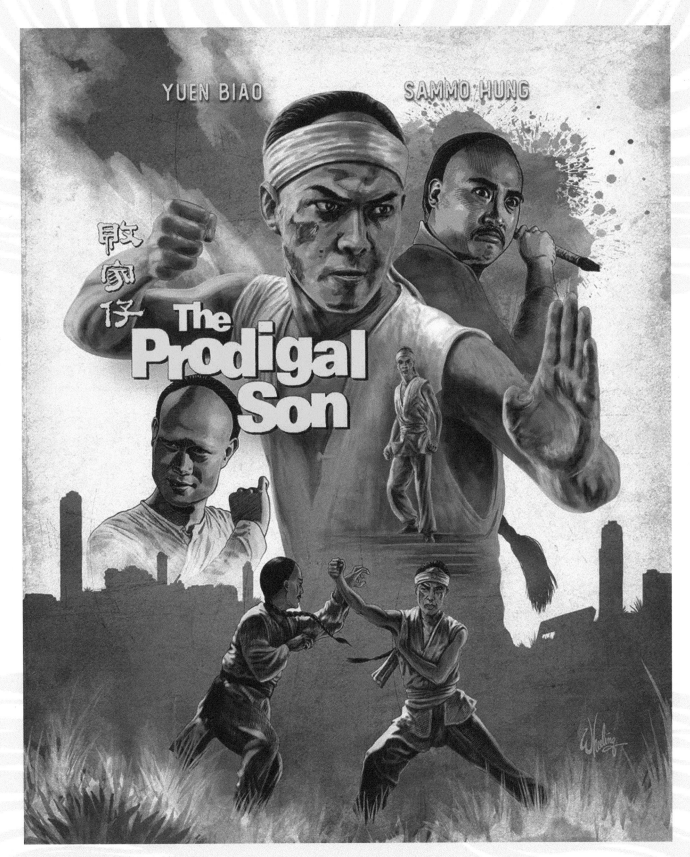

YUEN BIAO   SAMMO HUNG

The Prodigal Son

the blue, purple, and black mix, really works. Whilst the fashion now seems to be pastel colours and minimalist design, what influences your drawing and colour style?

DW: When I walk down the grocery store aisle I'm bombarded with shelves of products all vying for my attention. I look at what works for me, what doesn't, and why. I can't go shopping and not pay attention to the design that went into the packaging. It's often the best part, but also sometimes the part that sadly gets thrown out. It's a fun challenge to design something with multiple purposes: It needs to grab attention on a store shelf (or tiny website thumbnail), stylistically

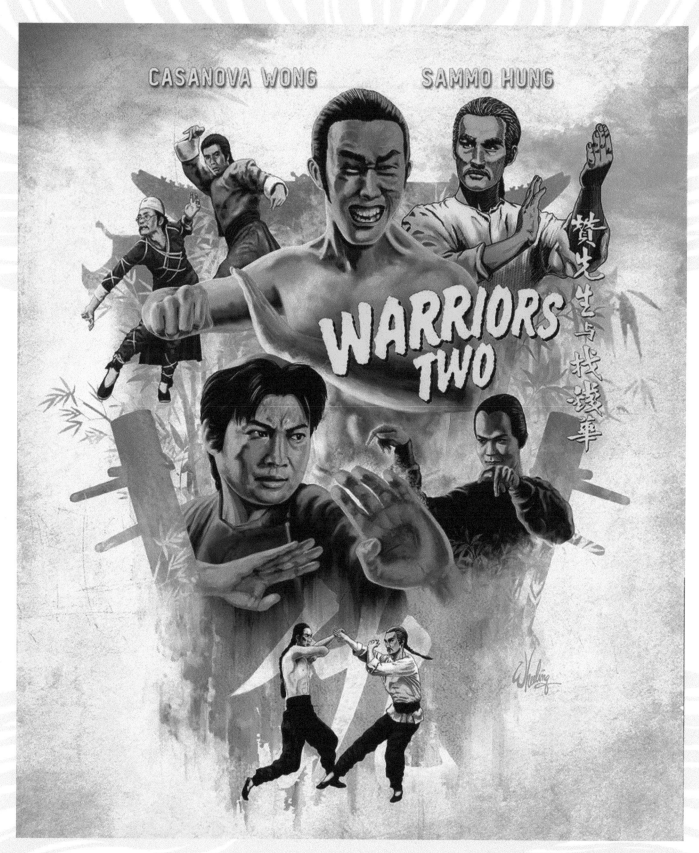

conveys its thematic contents (horror, kung fu, love story) and also function as an attractive container the user wants to keep and perhaps even display on their home shelf. All while doing this in an art style that is true to the period of the film.

1960s films were typically marketed with hand-painted posters. 1990s films were typically marketed with photo collages. So I do my best to package the film in a style congruent to the time the film was made.

SP: We're so proud and honoured for you to have created the cover for this edition of Eastern Heroes magazine. The Bruce Lee drawings are unreal, how long does it take to create each drawing?

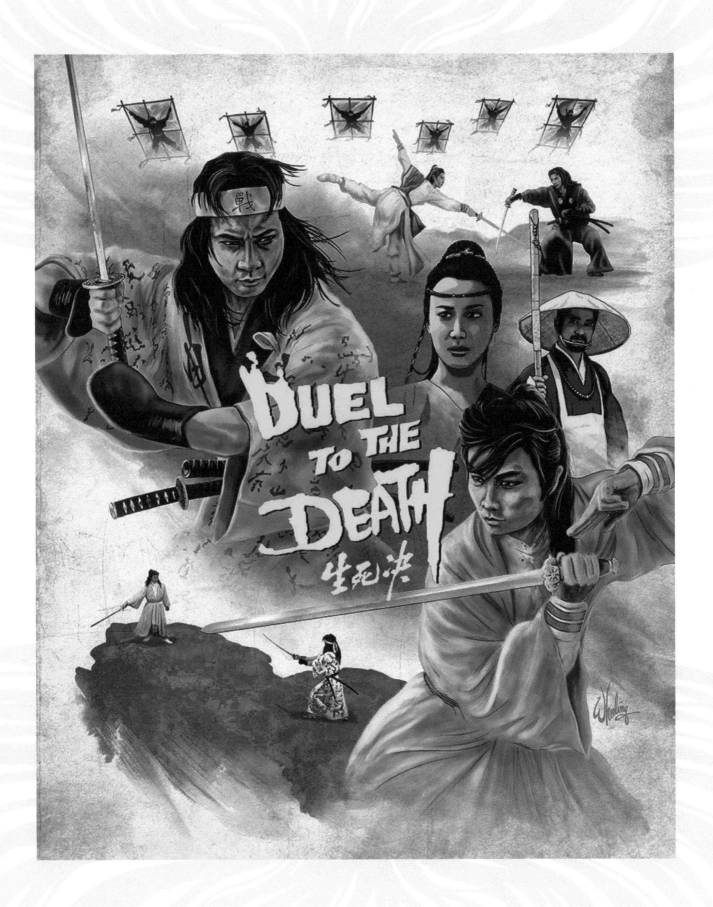

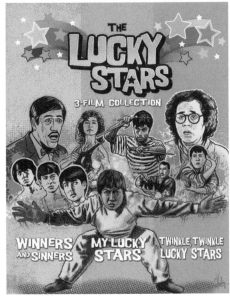

DW: It's weird, or maybe not, but I totally lose all sense of time when I get into a drawing project. And that's the way I like to work. No distractions and just draw all day. But it's rare I get that luxury. I usually have multiple projects going on at once. Phones ring. Clients want something. The dog wants something. (Luckily my pet turtles are pretty chill.) But there are endless distractions. So it's hard to say how long it took me to do this cover if I could've done it without stopping. Maybe 7 hours.

SP: When you are not drawing martial arts film covers, what do you like drawing in your spare time?

DW: What is this "spare" time you speak of? Ha. Since I got my little Westie dog, I don't do much free time drawing anymore. But when I did, I normally drew in a more cartoony style than you see on these movie covers. Honestly, it's more fun, casual and free-flowing. I don't have to care about accurate anatomy or Bruce Lee's arm veins. I wrote a comic book in 1987 that I didn't finish illustrating. I still have it and have toyed with the idea of finishing the art for it now. Thirty-five years later. It would be a fun exercise to draw it in the same style I did in 1987, blending the old with the new pages. And since it takes place in 1987 I would approach it as a "period" piece now. Making certain to draw furniture, phones, cars, and fashion as it existed then. If I had the time and didn't have to worry about income, I might do that.

SP: Do you have any future projects coming up you wish to talk about?

DW: I just do my job the best I can, get paid and hopefully learn something from each project. I let my clients make their announcements when they are ready. That's THEIR job. (Or the job of Amazon UK. Ha ha. They are known to sometimes leak release info.) I may have some things in the works, but I feel I've used up enough of your ink today.

SP: Lastly, thank you for the awesome cover and for talking with us; do you have any last words?

DW: When the labels ask what titles you want to see them release, use that opportunity to voice your desires. Not everything is available for them to put out, and not all old HK films have yet been remastered in HD, but they DO listen and continue to release the best of what's available. And a big "THANK YOU" to EASTERN HEROES for chatting with me, and keeping the Hong Kong Action Cinema fires burning! Carry on!

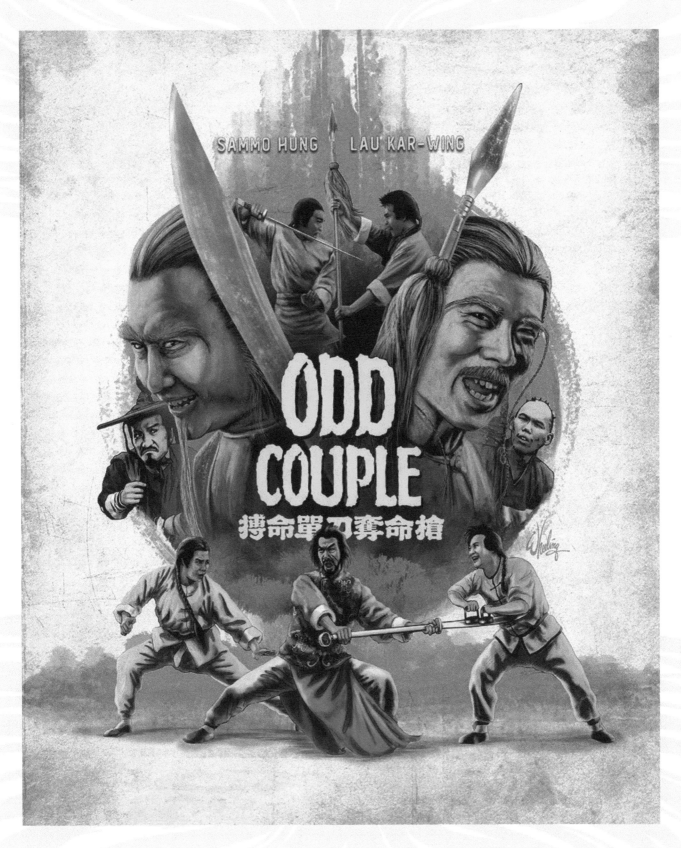

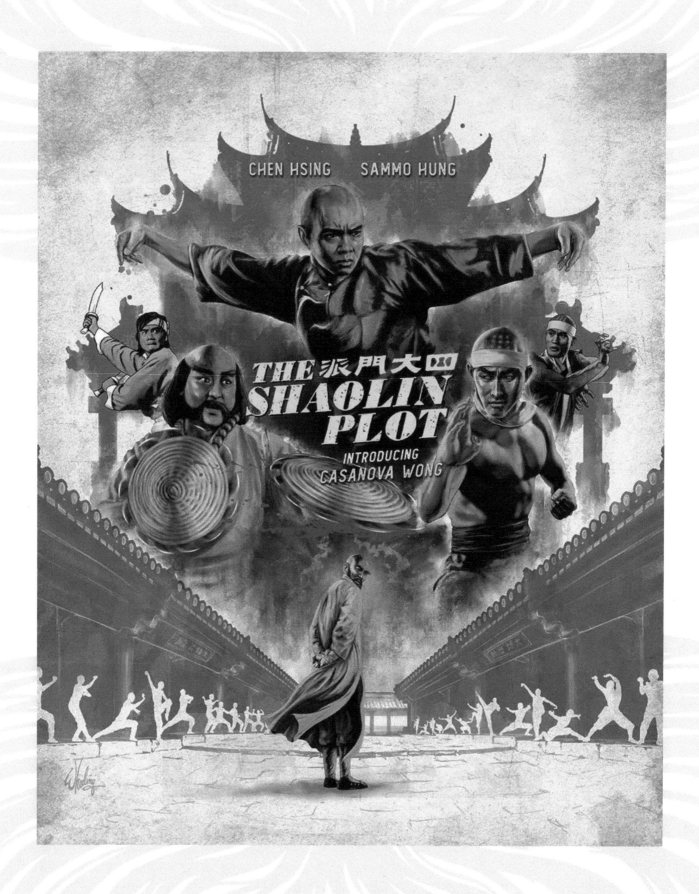

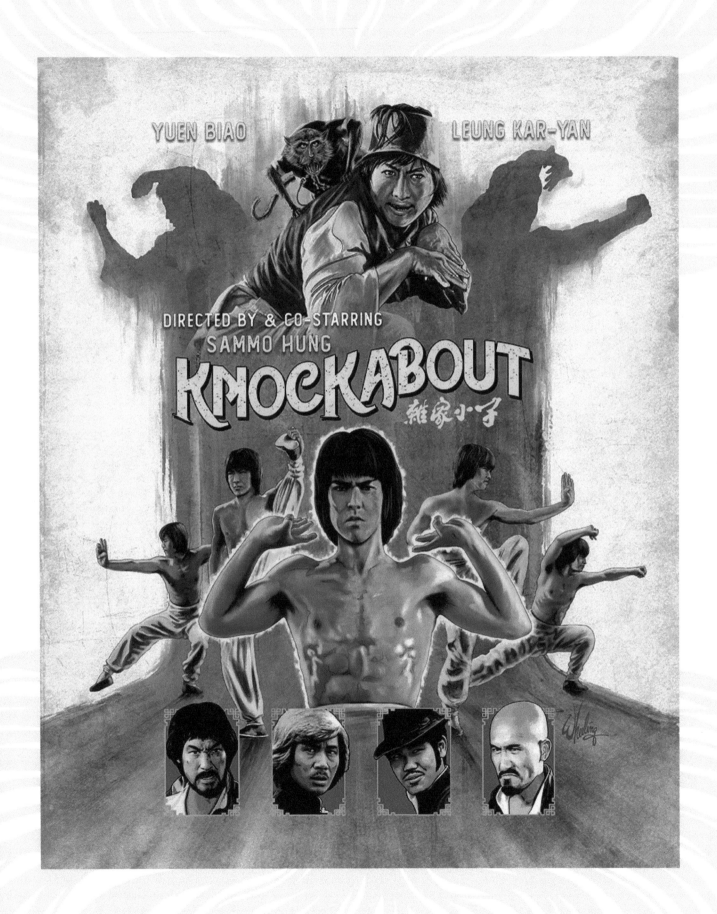

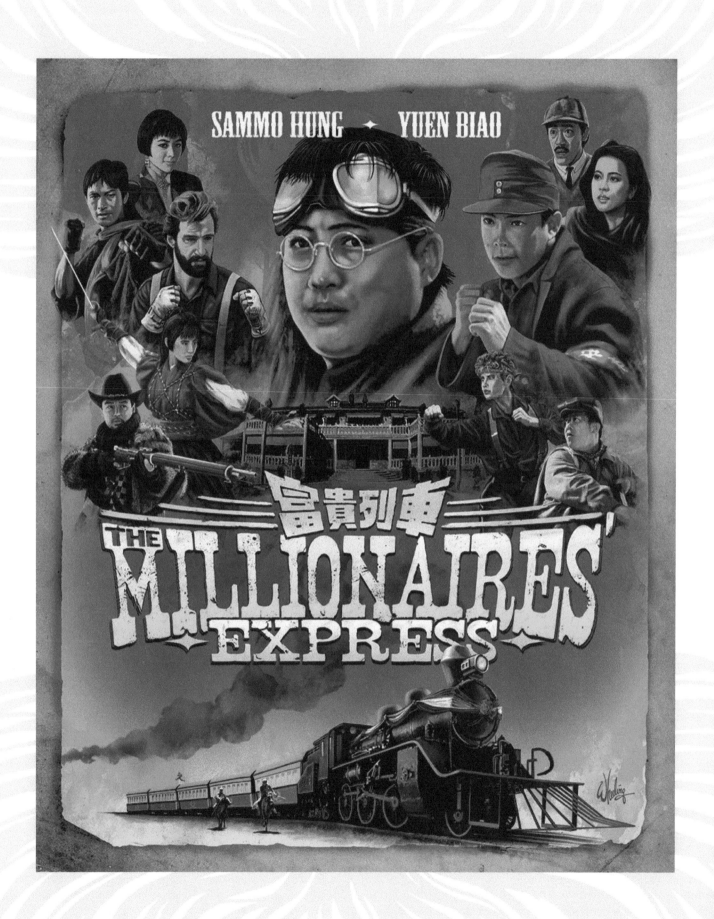

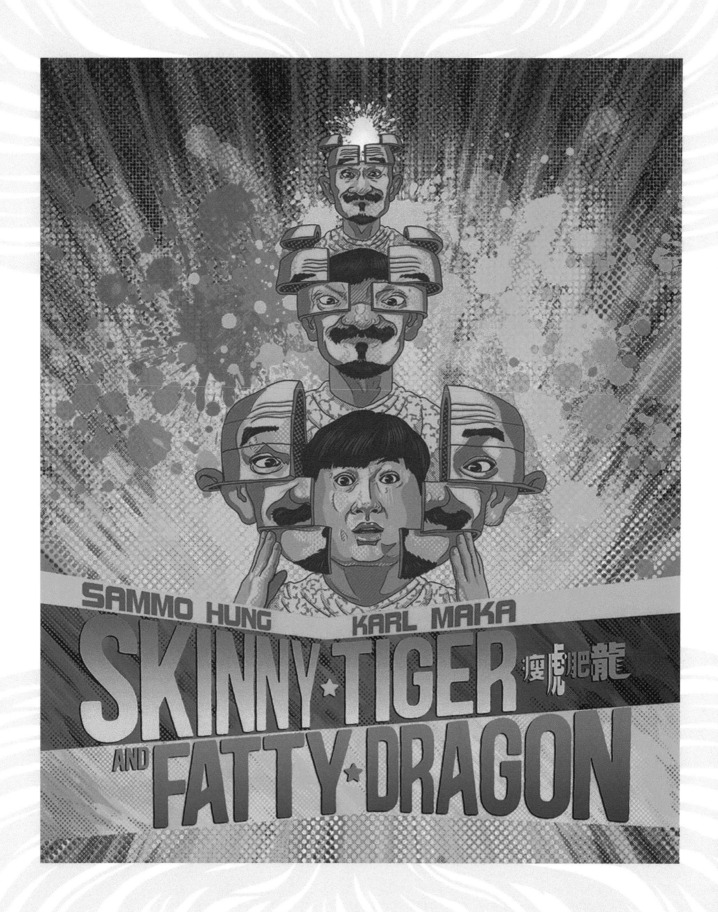

ONCE UPON A TIME IN CHINA TRILOGY

黄飛鴻

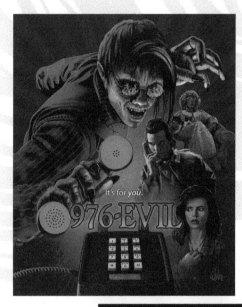

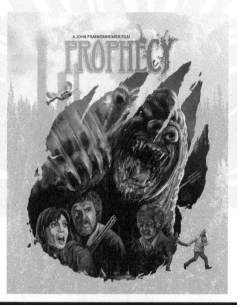

36 DEADLY POSTER STYLES

With Alan Donkin & Matt Routledge

After milking the teats of poster collectors for the last three issues, I can't really justify yet another cop-out on my part. I guess I was due to put in some actual effort in this series about Asian cinema posters. What could I write about, though? After listening to the recollections of the many collectors featured, I recalled one particular comment that caused me to halt the editing job and take a moment to think. Jared King is to blame. Over the years I have developed a curiosity about the design distinctions between posters in different territories. Jared said that he preferred film posters from their 'home' territory. It's a straightforward enough statement – if a film was produced in Hong Kong, then Jared prefers the Hong Kong poster.

It was a comment that pinged around my head like a ball-bearing on a cheap pinball table. Did I agree? I didn't know whether I did or not. My mind grasped at fuzzy, half-remembered mental images of Thai posters for HK releases, desperately trying to shape an opinion. Jared admitted that he was perhaps being a 'snob' about it – which is one letter more than the word I've exclaimed when I've read his 'ok' rating of some of my most-revered classic films. Perhaps he was right, though? The thought expanded in my head like my waistline during lockdown. I wanted to find out. How best to go about it, though? A few ideas started to take root. Firstly, it seemed prudent

to limit the time frame involved. There are thousands of film posters out there, and it's not really an achievable goal to examine them all in a magazine article. A broad look at different styles in the 'classic' era

COLD WIND HANDS

is a reasonable aim to pursue. Sorry, Jared. I won't be looking at your heroic bloodshed favourites. Secondly, once the whistlestop tour was complete, I thought it would be interesting to look at a single film, and compare its

posters directly. A case study, if you like. This approach certainly has its pitfalls – some films have wildly different posters, whereas others seem more uniform. Nevertheless, it's something that may illustrate subtle, as well as obvious, similarities and differences. Thirdly, I thought that my ramblings could benefit from an additional perspective. After our enjoyable collaboration in the Jackie Chan special issue, I asked Matt Routledge if he would work together with me on this piece, and he graciously accepted.

MR: Only with a gun to my head, 'Chow Yun Fat' style, and the promise of Alan's poster collection swiftly arriving at my house.

AD: I must have zoned out during that conversation. Anyway, wishful thinking aside, the whole writing process has been a dialogue between Matt and me, so without further ado, we present our findings. Disclaimer: there aren't 36 styles of poster. But there are a lot. Welcome back, Matt. I bet you've been counting the days down until our next collaboration?

MR: Those Wang Yu posters never arrived, so I have been waiting for you to honour our deal of putting your hands in the hot stones whilst I sip a green tea and watch Challenge of the Masters (1976) on repeat.

AD: What sordid fantasies you have. I thought I'd ask for your input in this matter, although I'm beginning to regret it already. You've been a collector for a lot longer than me, so I'm hoping that together we can take a decent look at what's out there. And possibly take down Jared King.

MR: I promise to make this a clean, smut-free contribution (unlike Jared).

AD: To start with, how about we look at poster designs by territory? What do you reckon? Hong Kong from the late-1960s to the mid-1980s? The so-called 'old school' era.

MR: What a fantastic iconic era that was! Too many classics to mention. Straight off the bat from the early days we have The Chinese Boxer (1970), One Armed Swordsman (1967), Come Drink with Me (1966), Vengeance (1970) - the list goes on and on! Let's tuck into some hand-drawn masterpieces that deserve more attention.

AD: Traditionally, I have been slightly less than knowledgeable with regard to Hong Kong posters. I convinced myself a while back that movie distributors only seemed to put out hand-drawn posters to accompany their epics. You know the type. Not-quite photo-realistic, but not far off it. Sketched, and with huge faces bursting from a background of action poses. Massive block text to indicate the EPICNESS of the film.

MR: Have to be honest, I absolutely love the hand drawn 60s and 70s movie posters. Even to this day, they are some of my absolute favourites. Hand-drawn seems to be very much a thing of the past, so these posters firmly marked the era that they came from through this unique style.

AD: Let's concentrate on that late 60s/early 70s era. Shaw Brothers nailed the style during this early window of our period. A few spring to mind. The Assassin (1967) is an excellent example. Note the dominance of Jimmy Wang Yu above

all others, the totem pole of secondary characters, and the action scene in the bottom left. It's a classic poster – even the block writing has cracks in it to signify… actually, that's a point. What does it signify?

MR: That Wang Yu is 'well ard' basically and can crush it with his rock solid abs. A great poster: colourful, eye-catching, and with a great 'I am about to kill you' pose from Wang Yu dominating the centre.

AD: Note the yellow to red background, too. Chaos. Carnage. Blood. All are suggested by this very simple gradation of colour. I get the feeling that every element of these hand-drawn posters was carefully considered and controlled in order to present a very specific image to the potential punter.

MR: Agreed, and the 3D-style block lettering of the title makes a distracting appearance, repeated several times years later by Shaws on other titles such as Boxer Rebellion (1976).

AD: Wow, a landscape poster. We'll talk about those later. Another incredible example of Shaw's approach to movie posters is Twelve Deadly Coins (1969). No totem pole this time, but a towering central image of a sketched Ching Li, accompanied by a couple of battle scenes below. These veer into cartoonish territory, with faces and stances appearing somewhat vague. This lends the scenes a certain energy that really works for me. The background in this poster is beautiful, using washed-out greys, greens, blues and purples to suggest a colder atmosphere than The Assassin.

MR: It's a cracker and a highly sought-after poster. The yellow lettering really stands out and it's a lovely piece of artwork, with one of Shaw Brothers' most beautiful actresses, Ching Li. For me, this has the edge on The Assassin, but I do love both equally for their aesthetic qualities.

AD: Those Shaw examples are ten-a-penny. There are dozens of examples of martial arts film posters that fit a similar design bracket. I haven't seen one yet that I dislike. Look at Brothers Five and Swordswomen Three (both 1970). So good I could cry. Damn you, Jared.

MR: Two sterling pieces, Brothers Five and Swordswomen Three. I am going to give you a rare flattering comment and say great choices there. But this still doesn't mean I let you off the hook with the hot stones thing.

AD: Carter Wong's knuckles look like he's been braying a boulder for twenty years. Mine look like I've been washing dishes using mild green Fairy liquid for the same length of time. The hot stones might develop my toughness cred (which currently stands at zero). Moving on … linking back to what I said earlier, I soon discovered a fatal flaw in my theory about Hong Kong's posters of the late 1960s/early 1970s being hand-drawn only.

MR: Is the flaw that the theory was absolute guff?

AD: That's right. It was twaddle. I present Exhibit A – The Boxer from Shantung (1972). There's at least two versions (white and black) and Chen Kuan-Tai's black and white photograph is the focal point of both of them. Exhibit B, from the same

year, is Delightful Forest, which features a lot of photographs, and even a nice copy and paste job to showcase a sideways kick. It's a nice poster, but that kick is a bit too cheesy for me. Are you a fan?

MR: Full respect to Ti Lung, though. On the Delightful Forest one, if you look carefully, he is on the poster five times. Surely that's a record for a movie poster! And that Shaws logo is huge! Not complaining, but it's rare to see the logo that big on one of their posters. Not a fan of the cut and paste style they did, but it's interesting to compare that style with other films released around that time in the early 70s.

AD: The fact that these are both Shaw Brothers films proves to me that hand-drawn art wasn't a 'non-negotiable'. I would argue, however, that it was their signature style over this period, and that anyone wanting to see high-quality movie

THE
BOXER
FROM
SHANTUNG
IN EASTMANCOLOR

SHAW SCOPE

A CHINESE PICTURE WITH ENGLISH SUBTITLES

poster artwork should investigate their output further.

MR: And what an output that was! Shaw Brothers made well over 1000 titles. That's a lot of incredible poster artwork to hunt down.

AD: I'm sure you've got a few spares you can send my way as compensation for your insults and violent fantasies. I think it's worth stressing that Shaw Brothers weren't the only Hong Kong studio producing hand-drawn art over this period. Story of Thirty-Six Killers (1971) by the Jia Cheng Motion Picture Company is a fabulous example, and, of course, Golden Harvest's The Big Boss (1971) and Fist of Fury (1972) are familiar to genre fans.

MR: Absolutely, Golden Harvest had some incredible posters for their movies. Tattooed Dragon (1973), Shaolin Plot (1977), Hand of Death (1976), Broken Oath (1977) and One-Armed Boxer (1972) are all super hand-drawn examples of 1970s Golden Harvest posters. Warriors Two (1978) being a personal favourite poster of mine from the late 70s era.

AD: Hmm. Can you remember the bit where I mentioned the focus being the early 1970s period? I'm trying to keep everything focused and precise, and yet here you are, Mr. Film Director, going off-piste willy-nilly.

MR: I'll just look up 'control freak' in the dictionary.

AD: Order, order! Unwilling to let my pet theory go, I stupidly sought to justify it by looking at Taiwanese posters. Taiwan seemed to produce a huge amount of sketched poster art over the period. Look at Swallow Knighthood (1968). It's a pretty damn fantastic piece of work. Similarly, The Great Duel (1971) is stunning.

MR: Next Level. Some of the Taiwanese ones were even better than the Hong Kong versions. What would sometimes be frustrating is that the posters were five times better than the actual movies themselves, but somehow did a superb job in persuading the prospective viewer to go the theatre and watch the movie. Standouts include Seven to One (1973), Cold Wind Hands (1972) and The Fast Fists (1972).

AD: Oh, for the love of…! Actually, let's pause for a moment, if we can. The 'home version' Invincible Sword poster. I've already described it as a belter, but is it the best? The Thai version. Better or worse? What do you think? A King-Slayer?

MR: Very interesting one. Anyone who read our previous article will know how much we both love Thai movie posters, but for Invincible Sword, the Hong Kong version clearly wins.

AD: What? Explain yourself, sir!

MR: I'm not keen on the central image they used of Wang Yu in the Thai one, and then it gets a bizarre sepia look. The Hong Kong one is simple, yet effective (who said that line in a famous film?!). Wang Yu movies have some truly great posters in Thailand. Check out the incredible landscape ones for The Last Duel (1972) and The Chinese Boxer (1970). Knock outs!

AD: Stop trying to distract from your wrongness! I'd say that the Thai one was better. Don't get me wrong – I love the 'home' poster. It's tranquil, elegant, and really showcases Wang Yu's star presence. However, there's something about the Thai poster that I prefer. You know I'm a sucker for the sketched stuff, and that poster is such a

powerful, busy montage of portraits and action, it just blows me away. The sepia image isn't the greatest, I admit, but it's certainly striking. The poster in general is a beautiful piece of artwork. The horizontal design is something that seems more common in Thai posters than Hong Kong and Taiwan.

MR: I can prescribe you some glasses, Alan, if you need them? If they changed that sepia image, I would say it stood a great chance of being the superior poster, but it doesn't work for me this time round. We will agree to disagree on this one.

AD: Fair enough! So, Thai landscapes. Off the top of my head, I can think of The Rage of Wind, Enter the Dragon and Fist of Unicorn (all 1973) that are presented in a horizontal style, but a quick check through my photo albums revealed dozens. I only have a couple of 'landscape' posters from the classic era from Taiwan – Big Land Flying Eagles (1978) and Twelve Baldheaded Beauties (1979). What do you make of the style?

MR: Super dooper! I love the fact that they did landscape versions as well as vertical ones in Thailand. A bizarre

AD: That last one sounds like something from another genre. Oh no, I've gone full-Jared. Getting back on topic … as ever, the vaguest piece of research proved me completely wrong. Jimmy Wang Yu's The Invincible Sword (1971) is just one massive photograph. To be fair, it's a belter. It's a Golden Harvest production, but was filmed in Taiwan, which potentially muddies the waters. So, let's look at a more clear-cut example. The Magnificent Chivalry (1971) features another massive photograph of Wang Yu. It seems like the primary designs of the late 60s/early 70s in Hong Kong and Taiwan were the hand-drawn ones. To be honest, they are still my favourites.

MR: Wang Yu had some tremendous Taiwanese poster variants. The Hero (1971) is superb, as is Knight Errant (1973)…

AD: AND in the correct time period!

MR: …and Deadly Silver Spear (1977).

exception to the rule in the Shaw Brothers catalogue is the one I mentioned earlier - they released a rare Hong Kong landscape version of Boxer Rebellion (1976). But normally, they are mostly vertical designs. Big Land Flying Eagles we can agree to agree on – it's a terrific poster, and I love the way it uses the wider canvas to show the hordes of soldiers racing towards us on horses. Very visually striking.

AD: It's amazing. I'm very pleased to have both variants. Another feature of Thai posters that seems to be rather unique is the yellow border at the top or bottom of the image. I've only ever seen them

on Shaw Brothers posters, but I stand to be corrected. I have no idea what their purpose is, but they make the posters look quite striking. They often incorporate a little blue square saying 'Union Odeon', which I figured could be the theatrical distributor of Shaw films. However, it is also visible on the Invincible Sword poster,

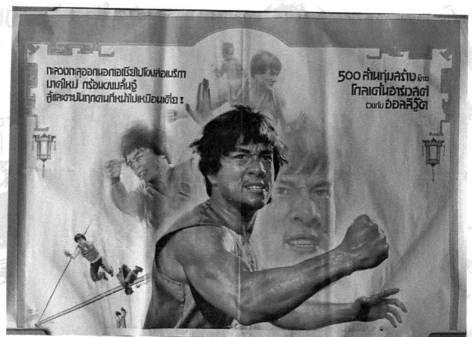

which is a Golden Harvest production, so maybe it's a more general distributor. Perhaps they used in-house artists to produce the artwork for the films they had imported to show in Thailand? I'm not sure that I've seen it on many posters after the mid-70s.

MR: Quite common on some Thai posters, I remember seeing it on the Thai poster for Odd Couple (1979).

AD: Embarrassingly, I have that poster.

MR: You are too busy dropping your jaw at the hand-drawn art to notice the finer details, Alan.

AD: Er, yeah. What do you make of the double page posters from Thailand? I've only got one – Battle Creek Brawl (1980) – although I'm aware of a few others. Game of Death (1978) seems to be very hard to find in its complete form. People just seem to have thrown away the left half, which is extraordinary.

MR: Very similar to the Japanese giant 'B0' posters which were so huge that they had to be joined together in two segments. As long as you have the other half, you are okay. Otherwise, it's probably a nightmare to track down half of an already scarce poster in the first place.

AD: Some posters from Thailand seem to have a very distinctive slightly cartoonish style. Perhaps from the late 70s onwards,

generally? It seemed to become the dominant style. I'm not sure 'cartoonish' is even the correct phrase. There's a definite attempt to replace a photograph with a painting. And then add a load of extra stuff in the background. A good example is Snake in the Monkey's Shadow (1979). The central pose is the same as the 'home' poster, but the rest is wholly different. The 'title' characters of the snake and monkey are afforded a far more prominent role on the Thai poster. One of the boons of creating a painting, compared to a montage of photographs. Another King-Slayer?

MR: Errr, Alan, that poster is Dance of the Drunken Mantis, not Snake in the

Monkey's Shadow. Can I officially fire you from your own article now?

AD: Huh? What are you talking about?

Do you think it's a Jared-Destroyer, or not?

MR: What are you doing still here? You can't mix up Dance of the Drunken Mantis and Snake in the Monkey's Shadow - two true genre classics - and expect to get away with it!

AD: I haven't! Do you need those glasses back?

MR: …

AD: Oh. I have, haven't I? This is … even more embarrassing than the Odd Couple mess up a few minutes ago. You're right! I deserve to be fired!

MR: Remember. Stay focused and be precise. You've made me sound like a kung fu teacher now.

AD: Ahem. Moving onto the next time period: the late 70s and early 80s. We had some truly cartoonish 'home' issues, didn't we? Drunken Master (1978) is a pretty well-known example. Are you a fan?

MR: Love it, fantastic poster! Gutted that, to this day, I have never found an original version of it. They had some crazy cartoon-esque large heads on some

of the Seasonal Movie poster artwork. If No Retreat, No Surrender (1986) came out in the 70s, I'd be interested to see what artwork the movie would have had! Drunken Master has such a fun and likeable image, but I am also very biased and swayed by the fact that I truly love that particular movie. All time classic!

AD: I appreciate the artwork. There's something about the caricature posters that leaves me feeling a bit empty, though. I'm not sure if it's due to that fact that my tolerance for goofball 'comedy' in the old school flicks has worn thin. Once upon a time I'd tolerate it in order to get to the shapes. I'd even force a laugh to try and sail through those scenes. There's only so much you can take, though, of an arrogant goon with a whiny voice and a mole on his cheek (and accompanying massive hair protruding from it) pulling stupid facial expressions. This style of poster seems to play up the scenes I find most tiresome, so maybe that's why I don't care for them a great deal.

醉拳

監製 吳思遠

導演 袁和平

（蛇形刁手第二集）

成 龍
袁小田
黃正利

領銜主演

武術指導 袁和平 徐蝦
攝影 張海
製片 張權

DRUNKEN MASTER

香港思遠影業公司出品　SEASONAL FILM (H.K.) CORPORATION

MR: It's Drunken Master!!! and you are overruled.

AD: I can't deny that it's a classic. Let's move on. That daft theory I had was clearly wrong, but I would say that perhaps HK/Taiwan posters in the late 70s/early 80s featured more photographs than hand-drawn artwork.

MR: I will be honest, I'm not a fan once the cartoon images started slowly disappearing. It was the end of an era, and like anything in life, the posters had to evolve, I guess. But it's great to look back fondly now on the 60s and 70s hand drawn posters and give them the acclaim and respect they truly deserve.

AD: Pearl Chang's My Blade, My Life (1978) uses a lot of photographs to present its cast. It's like a game of Guess Who? It's got a pleasing font colour and background, but it's a bit too busy for my tastes.

MR: Not a fan, but it shows how the poster art was continuously changing.

AD: Cliff Lok's Choi Lee Fat Kung Fu (1979) is also very busy, but it feels like the design has better balance. With My Blade, My Life, the bottom half was like a football crowd, but the montage on Choi Lee Fat spreads things around more.

MR: Perfect opportunity to talk to yourself here, Alan. I can't comment on these posters.

AD: That's interesting. Can I go all 'Dick Turpin' on you and demand that you surrender all your late 70s/early 80s photo-based posters? Stand and deliver, your posters or your life! As a sidenote, I find it amusing that you can clearly see the black trim lines around these photos, where they layered them on top of each other. I've grown to really like the photo montage ones. There's hits and misses, but when they work, they really work.

MR: Pfft.

AD: See what I have to work with here, people? Shall we shift to Japanese posters? There's some stunners in the archives. The Bruce Lee film posters are excellent.

MR: 100%. Look at that Big Boss (1971) beauty - a great montage with a brilliant

pose from Bruce. A great choice, I might add, as it's one of the stand-out scenes in the film. Japan seems to always know exactly how to construct a poster in the right way, and this Bruce Lee classic is no exception.

AD: Poster designers in Japan had a fine mastery of image/art/font balance. A lot of the posters produced in that country seem to take a unique spin on the source film, rather than recycle 'home' designs. One-Armed Boxer (1972) is a superb example of this. It's entirely different to the HK release.

MR: Love the One-Armed Boxer Japanese poster. Actually, it has two variants in B2 format, and both are terrific. Hong Kong stuck to the hand-drawn artwork, whilst Japan produced a hand-drawn version and one with actual images of key scenes of the movie.

AD: In a moment of

solidarity with Jared, I probably prefer the Hong Kong version. Annoying. I think it's the colour scheme of the Japanese version that doesn't click with me. There are too many contrasts. It's like the world as seen through the eyes of a 1950s invading Martian.

MR: The Hong Kong Poster is such an iconic image to me that I find it hard to be bettered, simply due to personal, sentimental value, but the two Japanese versions are fantastic alternatives.

AD: Other than the colour scheme, the balance of the poster is excellent. Nothing is too cluttered or top/bottom heavy. The text isn't too invasive. The selection of images is precise and exciting. Companies such as Toei released hundreds of yakuza and samurai flicks in the 50s and 60s. It seems like Japan's mastery of theatrical poster design was already in place by the time the kung fu craze arrived.

MR: The Japanese B2 posters of Sonny Chiba's Street Fighter series are great, particularly the rare B0 versions of Return of the Street Fighter (1974) and The Street Fighter's Last Revenge (1974).

An honourable mention must go to the 1975 Japanese B2 Bullet Train poster. I've always loved that design and its very striking yellow and dark-orange image.

AD: Japan also released multiple variants for the 'bigger' films. I know that The 36th Chamber of Shaolin (1978) has at least three different versions.

MR: Yes, but let's be honest. The Hong Kong version is clearly the definitive one for The 36th Chamber of Shaolin. It's a beautiful montage poster of an all-time classic movie.

AD: Totally agree. Another thing I'll say about posters from Japan during this era is that the paper quality is rather good. It feels weighty and glossy. Now, the final area we should look at in this brief tour is Korea. To me, posters from Korea are an enigma. They are scarce and there's not much information out there. I have a few in my collection, but my main source for them vanished off eBay a few years ago.

MR: I am not big on the Korean film posters, but from the ones I have seen from the 70s, there are some great designs.

AD: Have you noticed that a lot of them have 'Cinemascope' written on them? Very nice of them to essentially present the screen ratio on the theatrical posters!

MR: I guess it was a fad at the time, having a true widescreen film. Saying the word 'Cinemascope' somehow made the film feel bigger and added grandeur. Therefore, the audience were being told on the poster to prepare themselves for an 'epic.'

AD: Korean posters seem to have some very good designs in my opinion. I'd argue that the Korean version of Naked Comes the Huntress (1978) is better than the Hong Kong one. Seriously, who'd look at the 'home' poster and think, 'That looks cracking. I'll go and see that'?

MR: Jared ... definitely Jared. They obviously thought in the early 70s that sex sells, hence the scantily-clad beauty appearing on the poster. They obviously thought she looked better in the buff than the lead James Tien does. For me, I am

watching it for being a 'Golden Harvest' film with James Tien, but I am guessing you don't believe me?

AD: I don't. You'd only see it because it looks like it could be Category III. I really like the Korean designs. They're often unique representations of the films. Not always – The Angry Guest (1973) is a poster that's very similar to the original variant – but generally, there's some beautiful original artwork designs out there. I can see why the designs are too fussy for some. There's not a great deal of subtlety to them. One major drawback about Korean posters is that they are printed on the thinnest paper imaginable. Not even newspaper thickness in some cases. You certainly wouldn't wrap your fish and chips in them. They are like tissue paper. Not the stuff you keep in the bog – more like the stuff you used at school to make a collage. I think you can buy it in card shops and supermarkets now as a cheap-ass way to wrap gifts. The paper quality of these posters is appalling and may go some way to explaining why they are so rare.

MR: That's certainly a possibility.

AD: Ok, Matt. That's the overview completed. It feels like we've merely scratched the surface of a far deeper, more complex topic. Would you say you prefer 'home' variants?

MR: Definitely, when it comes to Hong

Kong films, yes. 100%.

AD: You two are like two peas in a pod.

MR: It's not just a design thing for me. Despite the versions of other countries sometimes being better, I feel that to have an original poster from the country it was originally made and released is the best for me, personally.

AD: I don't. I appreciate the sentiment. It's like singing Italian opera in its native tongue – it sounds wrong in other languages, no matter how accurate. But for me, the poster art itself overrules that. I don't necessarily think it's 'better' or more 'right' to have the home territory poster. For you guys, it seems to be matter of authentic preference. Whilst I appreciate that, I'd say that personally, it doesn't hold as much sway over me as the beauty of the design. I think there's good and bad examples of poster art in all territories, home or not. Shall we look at a case study?

MR: Let's.

AD: I was thinking of The Chinese Boxer (1970). It seems to have a uniform design that we can use to compare variants directly. The Hong Kong original. Absolute classic?

MR: Absolute classic! One of my favourite movie posters and a real rarity these days. Love the drawn images on this one, and the red and yellow combo is so visually striking.

AD: For me, it's a poster of two halves, with good and not-quite-as-good aspects. The colours are more earthy than the home variant. The landscape a design choice is great – it allows for a different arrangement of the key features. The classic image is still present, but less prominent. It's shifted over to the right and in full colour. The angle of it matches the Japanese variant. Mount Rushmore has gone. However, their facial expressions look jollier. That changes the tone of the film for me, and suggests less anger.

MR: The character pics are great, despite Lo Lieh's teeth-whitened cheesy smile. This poster has a huge amount of character, with superb hand-drawn artwork, and well-positioned images and text. I want it!

AD: I really like the suggested brawl in the background, beside a structure. It's the only poster of the three that establishes a setting. The text is nicely arranged. Especially the pre-Star Wars scroll in the top right. What I like about the Thai poster is the way that nothing hogs the image. Everything has its own place. Yet it's not a plate of separate items – they all combine to make a beautiful meal. Even the colours are riffs on shades of blue, red and orange. It's a stunning piece of work. Yet it lacks the visceral mood of the HK original.

MR: I just said I want it Alan, I can't elaborate any more than that!

AD: Chill, Verruca Salt. From what I know, there's only one known copy of the Thai poster. I can't even find the Korean version! All I've got is a newspaper advert. Thanks to Mathieu St-Pierre for the image. Presuming that the advert is very similar to the poster, it seems more stripped back than the Thai design. However, we can't include it, because it's just guesswork, and we can't see the colours.

MR: Hopefully one will surface one day.

AD: All three included variants are excellent. Agreed?

MR: 100%. You are definitely bidding against me if they ever land on eBay.

AD: I have to say, the powerful simplicity of the HK version is my favourite. It's the

AD: Hand-drawn art – check. Kinetic action shot – check. Mount Rushmore of characters – check. Balanced arrangement – check. Potent colour contrasts – check.

MR: If you want to put it like that. Just see them for what they are, and if they are great movies too, then that also makes me more biased in wanting to like the poster more.

AD: Ok, so what about the Japanese variant? We've got the same pose, pivoted about 90 degrees. It suggests the superiority of one fighter over another, which possibly imbalances the tone? Mount Rushmore has been flipped and

bleached with teabags. The colours are less striking. I have to say, though, that I really like the addition of the mass brawl at the bottom. It promises action on a more epic scale.

MR: I like the Japanese variant too, but much prefer the red look to the Hong Kong one. The 'Mount Rushmore' of characters, as you put it, is more striking on the Hong Kong version.

AD: You really have an issue with sepia! Let's talk about the Thai version.

MR: The Thai version is superb. I really love it, especially as it provides the movie with a rare landscape version.

THE FIVE VENOMS

red background, I think. We seem to have confirmed Jared's theory, despite my efforts to spend a whole article undermining it…

MR: No naked ladies, though, so he won't be bidding against us. Happy days!

AD: Just as a matter of interest, where do you stand on The Five Venoms (1978)?

MR: The Thai version, and only the Thai version. I will completely contradict what I said earlier. This movie is my exception to my 'only buy the Hong Kong movie poster from Hong Kong' rule. Just look at those colours and drawings on the Thai version. It's a cracker! I would still love to own the Hong Kong version, too, but it's second best for me for this title. I picked up the Thai version back in 2002 whilst in Bangkok and it has actually become quite a rare Thai poster to find these days. Hopefully everyone agrees it's worth trying to track down and would look superb in a frame.

AD: The Hong Kong variant is a masterpiece. I can't deny it. The

monochrome faces. The coloured silhouettes of the creatures. The action poses. The only thing I don't like is the orange to green colour blend. I feel like a bit of a heathen saying this, but I actually prefer the Thai design, as well. I'm saying that through gritted teeth, looking at my feet. I really am. Can I hear the rumblings of a lynch mob assembling? I'm sorry. I know it's garish, but it's just such a stunning patchwork of colours. I'm aware of the hypocrisy – orange colliding with green – but I can't help it! The action poses are more fully released, and the faces are so well-drawn. We are going to get pelters for this.

MR: I love the way you repeat what I say, just longeeeerrrrrrrr and more detailed.

AD: I've just shattered any credibility I had, haven't I?

MR: No, you did that earlier. Now, you've earned a brownie point in my book. But not a free poster, I might add. This has

been fun. I love any opportunity to look at a few great kung fu movie posters and put you down at the same time. This must continue!

AD: It has! Thank you for sharing your precise and focused thoughts! How much did Jared pay you?

MR: …………

Alan & Matt

THE WILD, WONDERFUL (AND COLLECTIBLE!) WORLD OF BRUCE LEE BOX SETS!

by Jason McNeil

Welcome, Fu Film Fans, to the first installment of what we here at Eastern Heroes have decided to call "THE VHS VAULT!" It will be a regular feature that digs deep into those days before streaming services vomited more movies than one could ever watch in six lifetimes right into our living rooms, and action and martial arts film fans were forced to haunt the shelves of the big chain and (even better!) local, Mom n Pop video stores, hoping against hope to spot a copy of The 36th Chamber of Shaolin or Battle Creek Brawl sitting on a bottom shelf, waiting for them to plop down their hard-earned, after-school job paycheck money and take it home to watch – after adjusting the tracking and putting up with a bit of popping and crackling, of course – in the privacy of their parents' living room! Or college dorm room. Or – y'know – what have you. (Hey! Some of us lived in a dojo in college and used to invite sexy co-eds over to watch movies and maybe check out how surprisingly soft the Judo mats were – but to each his own.....)

Of course, the boom of VHS (and the subsequent follow-up of DVD, after the face-plant that was Laser Disc....) proved to be a double-edged sword (which those of us who lived in a dojo liked to tell sexy college co-eds was called a jian in Chinese, as part of a vain effort to impress them with our restaurant menu level mastery of the language!) All that video store shelf space had to be filled with SOMETHING, and the 80s and 90s gave rise to the "Direct to Video" low-to-mid budget martial arts movie boom, that gave us heaping helpings of Cynthia Rothrock,

Richard Norton, Olivier Grunier, Jerry Trimble and even let Jean Claude Van Damme and Steven Seagal stretch out their careers far longer than mere big screen, theatrical releases would have allowed!

There remains a dedicated and vibrant sub-culture of movie fans who both crave and collect vintage VHS tapes, from Quentin Tarantino, who bought the entire inventory of Video Archives (the movie rental store he famously used to work at) when they closed, and currently does a massively popular and entertaining podcast based around watching those movies on VHS and talking about them, to cheap

bastards like myself, who just enjoy poking around secondhand stores, looking for cool stuff and delight in finding weird films on VHS that I didn't know existed, or haven't watched in years, or maybe that never even got a DVD or digital release and would be otherwise lost to the movieverse – usually for between 50 cents and one dollar US!

If you'd like to know more about the culture of rabid VHS collectors, there are a number of documentaries on several streaming platforms (which is weirdly ironic, now that I think of it), the best of which – at least that I've seen – is titled VHS FOREVER? Psychotronic People (2014.) It is streaming on Tubi and a few other channels, was directed by Darren James Perry and Mark Williams and features a chap named Ricky Baker in the top-billed spot, holding forth on all things video cassette and fu filmish. Do yourself a favor and check it out!

Now, all that having been said......
BRUCE LEE!!!!!!

REWINDING THE DRAGON!!!

With the rapid expanse of video store shelf space in the 80s and 90s, the previously played out purveyors of "Brucesploitation" movies saw a second chance to peddle their wares! Not making new movies, mind you, but repackaging and reselling (and, hopefully, re-renting and re-renting and re-renting again) the "mostly entertaining films of varying quality and budget" that they had cranked out in the 1970s. And if one Bruce Lee movie was good, then two was better, right? How about a boxed set, of three or four or even five Bruce Lee movies? OK, technically it was one Bruce Lee movie, and one Bruce Lai movie, and one weird movie with Bruce Li and a bunch of clips from Longstreet....

So, here we find ourselves, faced with the possibly awesome, possibly painful and most likely "some combination of the two" task of reviewing FOUR vintage BRUCE LEE BOXED SETS that have found their way into our collection. (Wait a minute. Why am I using the "royal we?" MY collection.)

I feel that the only way to approach the imminent Brucesploitation on video

cassette marathon is with some mentally lubricating libations firmly in hand. And in mouth, on tongue and eventually making their way thru the bloodstream into the brain. A brain which will, no doubt, be overwhelmed, amazed and delighted by the 70s Brucesploitation repackaged as 80s rentable and collectible awesomeness, via

the VCR that I bought from Goodwill for $15 - and then had to spend another $35 on Amazon to get adapters so I could hook the damned thing up to my big screen digital TV!

Come along with me, dear readers, and I will share the skinny on four of the best/ most collectible Bruce Lee Box sets (which you can hop on eBay and get for yourself, if you're so inclined!) AND the drink recipes for the martial arts themed cocktails that helped me along the journey. Its up to you whether you take part in one, the other or both.....

Here we go....

BRUCE LEE KUNG FU MARATHON!

Contents:
• The Real Bruce Lee
• Chinese Connection
• Fist of Fear
• The Man, the Myth

First of all, we've got four movies on two cassettes, so I'm assuming the picture quality isn't going to be that great, but – hey! - its old VHS, so its not like we're watching 4K.

Before we go any further, let's mix ourselves up the first of what will be, I'm assuming, several cocktails for the evening. For this one, an Emerald Dragon seems appropriate.

Emerald Dragon
2 ounces of vodka (I like Absolut)
1 ounce Chambord or raspberry liqueur
5 ounces of blue curacao

Combine in a shaker with ice, stir with Bruce Lee's speed and ferocity and strain into a chilled glass. That having been accomplished, on to the movies.

First up, The Real Bruce Lee.

Weirdly titled since its kinda the real Bruce Lee, but not really and then a couple of other wanna-be Bruce Lees and.....

Wow!

"Starring Bruce Lee and Introducing NEW SENSATION DRAGON LEE!"

Obviously cobbled together from vintage Bruce footage and other, lesser films, this thing has 42nd Street and the Deuce back in the day written all over it.

Brucesploitation at its Brucesploitation-est!

The first 30 minutes is literally old, childhood movie footage of Bruce Lee from Kid Cheung, The Bad Boy, Carnival, Orphan Scam – mostly Bruce running errands for the Triads. Even then, however, the young dragon's charisma is undeniable. Even in scenes where he's essentially a background character – the supposed Shermy to the rest of the Peanuts Gang – he still draws the eye and you find yourself not caring what the folks in the foreground are doing. Then, of course, we cut to the obligatory Bruce Lee funeral footage, followed by a voice over informing us that 'Imitation is the sincerest form of flattery!' before cutting to Bruce Lei doing what is essentially a 3 minute "action reel" fight in something called (and no, this isn't a typo) the JEEK KUNE DO DOJO! (Not sure where to even begin unpacking that one, so let's just pour ourselves a second Emerald Dragon and move on....)

The rest is basically a full length (albeit short length) film, originally titled Last Fist of Fury, starring Dragon Lee.

Ya gotta love that the movie is called The Real Bruce Lee and nearly ¾ of it is imitation Bruce Lees!

Dragon Lee does some weird fight scenes where he uses a long staff in the signature Bruce nunchaku style – which doesn't really fit – then sticks to the wall like Spiderman a few times, then bad guys in white ninja suits keep showing up and running away. I guess it was still a couple of years too early for Franco Nero or Mike Stone. Then he fights what appears to be Oddjob. Funny, but when he's not trying to be Bruce, Dragon Lee actually looks to have some serious skills, especially in the kicking area - looks very Tae Kwon Do-ish.

It seems odd, at first, that this cobbled together, unofficial sequel to Fist of Fury is on the tape BEFORE the movie it is a supposed sequel to. I mean, who watches part 2 before part 1, right?

After watching The Real Bruce Lee (aka some throwaway old Kid Bruce footage then Last Fist of Fury) the reasoning is painfully obvious. While its a fun, "so bad its good" watch in its own right – no one

with half a lick of sense would be able to stomach it right after the majesty that is the original Fist of Fury.

Chinese Connection

AKA Fist of Fury. A Bruce Lee Classic.

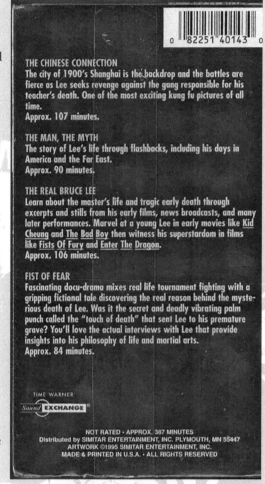

While this is the only actual Bruce Lee movie in the Bruce Lee Kung Fu Marathon of which we are speaking, the fact that you are reading Eastern Heroes tells me that you have already seen it multiple times, have reveled in its aforementioned majesty and don't need to hear me hold forth on it.

I did enjoy the rewatch, however. Dammed good stuff.

Moving on to VHS Tape 2.

Fist of Fear

Surprisingly, this is a retitled (or, more accurately, an abridged retitling) of one of my favorite, oddball Brucesploitation assemblages, Fist of Fear, Touch of Death. "Starring Bruce Lee, Fred the Hammer Williamson, Ron Van Clief," its a weird, cobbled together pseudo-documentary, built around Aaron Banks' 1979 Asian World of Martial Arts Tournament and Expo in New York City.

Banks put that tournament on annually for decades, and it was the best-known and – at times – most prestigious martial arts competition and show in America, eclipsed only by the Bermuda Nationals in the late 80s/early 90s. The footage of late 70s martial arts champs doing their thing and strutting their stuff on the biggest stage they could find is worth watching, in and of itself.

That having been said, the "plot" for the "documentary" is a network sports commentator named Adolph Caesar going up to the most famous martial arts people and action movie stars he can find in the audience (and Aaron Banks) and asking them "So, do you think Bruce Lee was murdered? Maybe with the Death Touch?" then listening to them give rambling, non-committal answers.

Fred the Hammer kicks a bit of ass, as well as "The Black Dragon" Ron Van Clief doing a full on martial master demonstration, before we cut back to the tournament footage, where the winner supposedly gets to be the Next Bruce Lee or inherit Bruce Lee's Mantle or something like that.

I'd tell you the name of the guy who won and was proclaimed "The Next Bruce

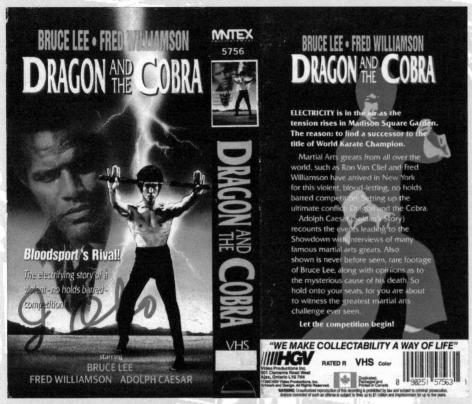

Lee, that does not skimp on the fights.

There are lots of fights. Lots and lots and lots of fights. Then, there are more fights.

Near as I can figure, the formula for this film was to travel to all of the cities, sites and locations that played an important part in Bruce Lee's life – essentially retracing the steps of the Little Dragon. Then, once they get there, a bunch of guys jump out of the bushes and he fights them. Then they move on to the next city.

The fact checkers were apparently on their lunch break during a few key moments, such as their declaration that Bruce "captured the Championship Title at the Long Beach Internationals!"

Excuse me, but that was Mike Stone.

Bruce did a cool demo, showed off his one inch punch and did some two finger push ups, and that impressed some people and got him the Green Hornet gig, but he didn't even compete in that tournament. Mike Stone did. And Mike Stone won.

However, the movie itself is a fun to watch fu-fest, with fists and feet flying pretty much non-stop.

Notable appearances include Ip Chun, son of Bruce's Wing Chun sifu, Ip Man, an early appearance by Yuen Biao as one of Bruce's many challengers, and a young Donnie Williams in the role of "Karate Thug!"

Well worth a watch, just for the fights and for the fun of it – although, be forewarned: While Yuen Biao's fight scenes are all kinds of awesome, his performance of Hung Gar empty hand forms looks like he's taking a particularly painful shit! (Which is kind of funny, actually, when you're six Emerald Dragons in.....)

WORTH A WATCH!

BRUCE LEE COLLECTOR'S EDITION

Contents:
• The Intercepting Fist
• Path of the Dragon

OK, both of these are clocking in at about 45 minutes each, so lets go with a libation

Lee" but I've forgotten it already. His 'fame check' must've bounced.

All in all, a fun watch, though. Worth checking out.

The Man, the Myth

Opening with some fake ambulance/ Bruce Lee on a stretcher footage, this looks like its going to be another cobbled together Bruce Lee "documentary," but it

is, in fact, a supposed Bruce Lee Bio-Pic.

While it occasionally gets closer to the facts of the Little Dragon's life than Dragon: The Bruce Lee Story (1993)... well, that's kind of a low bar, isn't it?

Let's start over.

The Man, the Myth (aka Bruce Lee: The Man, the Myth) is a 1976 loooooosely based on the facts biography film of Bruce

that lends itself to casual cocktailing and not power drinking for 6 ½ hours of Bruce Binge-ing (like last time!)

How about a Flaming Dragon?

Flaming Dragon
2 ounces of tequila
6 ounces of pickle juice
Texas Pete or other hot sauce
Sliced Limes

Mix tequila and pickle juice with ice and shake, then pour into a chilled cocktail glass. Garnish with a dash of hot sauce to taste and a lime twist.

The Intercepting Fist

An interesting documentary – apparently assembled in the mid-90s – featuring interviews and/or at least clips with Dan Inosanto, Taky Kimura, James Coburn and Peter Mark Richmond (also from Longstreet), George Lazenby, Mike James (who was then-publisher of Black Belt magazine), Rob Voss, John Saxon.... Lots and lots of good interview stuff in there, from people who knew Bruce Lee, worked with him and respected him.

It DOES pad its already short running time out by about a third with stock Chinese travel footage and wushu performances from the Shaolin Temple, and a BUNCH of clips from the Longstreet TV show (I'd love to know the backstory on how that happened.)

Altogether, worth watching.

Path of the Dragon

Hosted and narrated by Shannon Lee, this one combines a whole lot of clips from other 90s video store martial arts movie fodder – bits of fights with Richard Norton, Jean Claude Van Damme, Sammo Hung, Jackie Chan, Benny the Jet – with what appear to be unused pieces of the same interviews from the other one and some generic wuxia movie clips.

Frankly, it seems like they're trying to get a second feature out of the leftovers from the previous one, by framing it more in terms of "martial arts history" in general, instead of being just about Bruce Lee. Though they keep coming back to Bruce and, of course, his daughter is hosting it

and doing voice-overs.

A fair amount of Jackie Chan interviewing, though, and that's always fun.

The overall "theme" seems to be that Bruce Lee was the most important person, ever, in the history of the martial arts, because he was the "bridge" that brought a culturally restricted activity to the world at large, through the vehicle of his philosophy, martial arts skills, movies, general star power, etc.

Perhaps a valid point, albeit an arguable one, but worth discussing, none the less.

However.... near the end of the video, the purpose for making it suddenly becomes all too clear.

Shannon Lee interviews the documentary's "Producer, Writer and Director," one Walt Missingham, who basically lets the viewers know that all the history of kung fu has come down to him, personally, then claims to have been the first non-Chinese person EVER to have trained in the Shaolin Temple, back in 1983. Presumably thinking of her paycheck for the gig, Shannon Lee just nods along as he moves from one outrageous claim to the next.

Hey, Walt! Cynthia Rothrock, Dennis Brown and my first sifu, David White, were all at the Shaolin Temple in 1983,

as part of a training tour of American national martial arts tournament champions! I reached out to a few of them, and none I spoke to remember you. And, for the record, that was the SECOND training trip of American martial artists to China – I'm told that the first had been the year before, in 1982!

Producer/Writer/Director/Sifu/ Supreme Great-Grandmaster and Shaolin Pioneer Walt's bit of "end of the documentary" hubris aside, this boxed set is definitely worth watching. Obviously made for TV (with their 44 minute run times), the two docus would have worked better as one, but they're still a fun watch and worth checking out.

Recommended!

MARTIAL ARTS MADNESS – BRUCE LEE 5 PACK COLLECTOR SERIES

Contents:
• The Chinese Connection
• Fists of Fury
• The Legend of Bruce Lee
• A Dragon Story
• The Young Bruce Lee

OK, folks! Strap yourselves in, because this here is a long one! (Wait, this is Eastern Heroes! Thought I was writing for Honcho for a second. Take a moment, regroup, and....)

Silly double entendres aside, this is a five movie, five VHS cassette boxed set, so its going to take a hot minute to watch! To that end, let's mix ourselves a beverage that will both lubricate and energize our brain! I give you – The Bruce Lee Bomber!!!

The Bruce Lee Bomber
1.5 Ounces of Han Asian Vodka ("The only rice-infused, Asian vodka available in the United States.")
4 Ounces of Jackie Chan XGT Energy Drink (Alternately, Red Bull is acceptable)
Shot Glass
Rocks Glass

Pour half of the XGT into a rocks glass. Pour a big shot of Asian Vodka into a shot glass.
Drop the shot glass into the rocks glass.

Drink.
(Yeah, its a variation on an Irish Car Bomb.....)

The Chinese Connection (aka Fist of Fury) Fists of Fury (aka The Big Boss)

These are both noticeably better transfers than the films in the Bruce Lee Kung Fu Marathon – better colors and sound and, while its still a "pan and scan" edit, it fits a lot more nicely on the aforementioned widescreen TV. As VHS goes, these are among the better ones.

As before, I'm just going to assume that you've seen both these films more than once, so I'll spare you a walk through well-travelled terrain and get right to the "new stuff."

The Legend of Bruce Lee (aka Bruce, King of Kung Fu)

Starring Bruce Le and released in 1980, mere moments before Brucesploitation was about to give way to Ninjamania, this movie is.....

How to put it?

This movie is TOTALLY BATSHIT!

It starts with a meteor falling to Earth to mark the moment of Bruce's birth, and ends with Bruce learning Drunken Snake Fist Kung Fu to wreak vengeance on his vaguely motivated enemies.

(There is, however, a very excellent use of the term "Kung Foolery" which is now, officially, part of the Jas Lexicon. A Chinese astrologer explains to Bruce's dad about the Christ-like significance of stars falling from the heavens at the moment of his son's birth, to which Dad replies: "I don't believe in such Kung Foolery!")

Essentially, for most of the movie, Bruce just walks around town – mostly near college – and he keeps getting into fights.

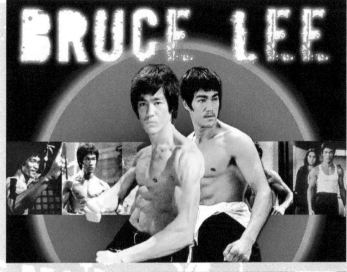

His dad sends him to learn Wing Chun, then he gets into more fights. Basically, rather than being "the Bruce Lee Story," this is a movie about a dumb teenager named Bruce who runs around Hong Kong doing dumb teenager things, gets into endless fights and occasionally breaks for a training scene.

The only high points of the movie are the unexplainable apprenticeship with the old master who teaches Bruce "Drunken Snake Fist Boxing" (which we ALL know

that the real Bruce Lee was a fan of, right?) and....

OK, how in the hell did they get both Bolo Yeung and Shih Kien to be in this thing?

Bolo just sort of runs thru it – blink and you'll miss him – but the final fight against Shih Kien actually delivers the goods! Even though, instead of Master Han's Hall of Mirrors, the battle takes place in a backyard somewhere, with Bruce busting out his newfound mastery of the Drunken Snake Fist Style, Shih Kien is – as always – outstanding, and elevates the battle... if not to the level of "must watch," then at least to "should watch." Shih Kien ALWAYS brings it – the guy had serious skills!

A Dragon Story (aka Bruce Lee: A Dragon Story)

I had to look it up – Directed by Ti Shih, starring Bruce Li and featuring an early appearance by Carter Wong (!!!) - because the opening credits are all in Chinese, with no subtitles, accompanied by a woman shrieking a song in Mandarin.

To call this a "bio-pic" is stretching the term to the breaking point. Its more like a "jazz riff" on Bruce Lee's life, but with fights and bad acting (and the occasional woman shrieking in Mandarin) instead of saxophones.

The film opens with Bruce, for some reason, delivering newspapers. Of course, a bunch of random guys jump out and attack him. And it goes on for awhile like that.

Hmmm.... This kind of falls into the "so bad it could be good" category, so.....

Here are a couple of the high points and "pluses" from A Dragon Story.

There is a scene – ok, get ready, because this is a lot – where a bunch of samurai (yes, samurai), in full Rashomon kit, show

BRUCE LEE

its hard to let go of the part where this one says that Linda Lee collapsed and DIED at her husband's funeral, and both bodies had to be flown back to Seattle for burial!

YUCK!!!

BRUCE LEE – THE LEGACY COLLECTION

Ok, we're going to break the rules a bit here, but trust me – its for your own good and you'll thank me later and all that sort of thing. (And Jay Lee will, doubtless, be outraged with me for going outside the parameters I previously set, but so be it.)

Shout Factory's Bruce Lee – The Legacy Collection was not released on VHS (it actually consists of 7 Blu Rays and 4 DVDs!) and has never, to my knowledge, sat on the shelf of a video rental store (it was released in 2013, and all the video stores were shutting down around 2010, when I moved to Hollywood – which made it a weird time to be breaking into the movie industry, but that's a story for another day....)

Still, if you're a Bruce Lee fan (and if you've read this far, I'm just going to assume you are), then you NEED to get this collection.

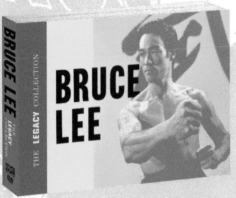

its very, very cool. I think I may need to dig around and see if the OST was ever dropped on vinyl.
A genuine LOL moment! Actual dialogue: "Chinese martial arts cannot be used for crime!" (The Hop Sing Tong and every bad guy Chow Yun Fat has ever fought would like to respectfully disagree.....)

The Young Bruce Lee

I see why they saved this one for last.

Also released in 1980. its the story of the titular Bruce and his apparent besties just sort of wandering thru a series of badly acted, melodramatic dialogue and bad fight scenes in front of a bunch of really photogenic landmarks – Buddhist temples, statue gardens, etc.

The pan and scan is TERRIBLE! Often, Bruce is talking and half his face is offscreen!

BONUS BADNESS: I know that Brucesploitation "bio-pics" play fast and loose with the actual facts of his life, but

First of all, it has The Big Boss, Fist of Fury, The Way of the Dragon and Game of Death, all digitally remastered on Blu Ray for your big screen, digital TV viewing pleasure - no $35 dollars worth of adapters required!

And the BONUS FEATURES! Oh, my dear lord, the bonus features will keep you entertained for hours!

And, since this set contains The Way of the Dragon, it seems appropriate that we settle in with a cocktail that I first encountered when a series of wrong turns led me into a sports bar across from a college in a tiny town in Southwest Virginia – the CHUCK NORRIS!!!!

Chuck Norris
1.5 ounces of Vodka
3-4 ounces of Red Bull (or, alternately, your favorite energy drink)
Grenadine
Fresh cherries
Texas Pete Hot Sauce (optional)

up in somebody's front yard and start attacking people with swords. Thankfully, "Linda" stops talking about how much she wants to get married and have kids just long enough to throw Bruce some nunchaku, and the kicking of the samurai asses commences.

Oddly, the movie has a really good jazz/funk soundtrack. I'm not sure if this was in the original (Hong Kong) edit or was added later for the 42nd Street crowd, but

Rocks glass. Pour Vodka and Red Bull into the rocks glass (over ice) and add a splash of Grenadine to taste.
Garnish with crushed cherries (think about it...) and a dash of Texas Pete (optional.)

OK – confession time.

Yeah, I'm in this one.

Not only did I help set up, arrange, film and even conduct a couple of the Bonus Feature interviews, I am featured in several BTS segments, holding forth on Bruce Lee as both a fan and... I believe I am technically credited as "Inside Kung-Fu Magazine Hall of Fame Writer of the Year." Something like that. (What can I say? Sounded better than "Rabid fanboy" or "Actor who one reviewer called 'the Ryan Reynolds of Direct to Video....")

In addition to some ramblings by my own blue-eyed self, the bonus features, BTS stuff and interviews abound, including in-depth bits with Dan Inosanto, Bob Wall, "Judo" Gene Lebell, "The Merchant of Menace" Anthony De Longis, bunches of others and, if memory serves, we even shot an interview with Rikki Rockett,, martial artist extraordinaire and world famous drummer for the rock band, Poison!

The cool bonus stuff just goes on and on.

Plus, there's even a book that comes with it.......
OK, I've gushed enough. Buy this and mark off a weekend to watch it all.

You'll be VERY glad you did.

• END OF SHAMELESS PLUG *

ABOUT THE AUTHOR:

Jason McNeil is an award-winning actor, martial artist and writer who learned kung-fu in the parking lot behind a Chinese restaurant while simultaneously holding down a second job at a video store called Moovies. This kind of set the stage for the rest of his life....

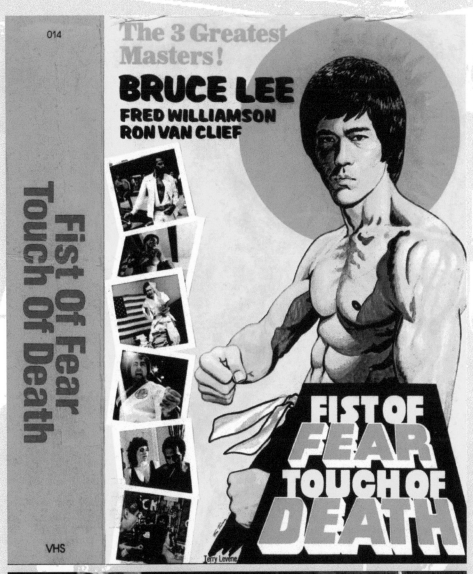

LONGSTREET

WAY OF THE INTERCEPTING FIST

By Simon Pritchard

Bruce Lee left Hong Kong to study in the USA in 1958 and then later pursue a career as an actor; one of his most notable roles was Green Hornet in 1966. One of Bruce's last TV appearances in the USA before returning to Hong Kong in September 1971 to film "The Big Boss" was "Longstreet", filmed in early 1971. The series has rarely been re-aired but appeared on the Canadian TV channel "Mystery TV" from 2005 to 2006. Longstreet was a detective show based in New Orleans (but filmed in LA) that aired on ABC in 1971 and lasted for one season (23 episodes) plus a TV movie. Longstreet was cancelled in 1972. The series starred actor James Franciscus as Mike Longstreet. James Franciscus is an established career spanning several decades. His work includes "Carlo" in "Cat 'o Nine Tails" (Dario Argento), "Alfred Hitchcock Presents" episode "Forty Detectives Later" and so much more.

Mike Longstreet was an insurance investigator who was blinded in an explosion that also killed his wife and is aided by his braille teacher, Nikki, and his guide dog, Pax.

The season consisted of 23 episodes with Bruce's character, Li Tsung, starring in four episodes intermittently throughout the series. The first episode aired of the series starred Bruce Lee was aptly named "The way of the Intercepting Fist".

"The way of the Intercepting Fist" - 16th

September 1971 - Episode 1.

In this episode Mike is coming to terms with his blindness and enlists the local antique store owner and martial artist, Li Tsung, to teach him to fight so he can take

revenge on the man that killed his wife and left him blind.

Li is first introduced when Mike is walking down a dark alley and three thugs attack him. The thugs hear a noise and one goes to investigate and he flies back into the rest

of them. Li is here! Li beats the other two thugs and they run back to their car and leave. Li tends to Mike and recommends he puts an ice pack on his stomach to relieve the pain. Mike asks who he is and Li introduces himself and leaves.

In the next scene, Li is with Mike at the Police station discussing who could be behind the attack; with Mike pressing the link that the thugs work for the gangsters who arranged his attempted murder, Li is the only witness who can identify the thugs. The Police offer Li private protection but he declines it. In this episode, Mike investigates the link between gangsters and crime at the local docks.

Mike later returns to Li's antique shop to persuade Li to teach him how to fight which Li initially declines. Li explains that he found the course of his ignorance to which Mike replies "Well, help me find mine!".

In the next scene, Li and Mike are training at Mike's house. Considering Mike's blindness, Li explains how to move the body as one whilst demonstrating to him. Mike starts by trying to kick Li in the stomach but he is shy and self-conscious, Li then asks Mike to hold the bag and kicks him so hard he flies about 10-foot back into his garden furniture. Mike loves it.

your eyes? A bird would attack without thinking..." Mike responds "I'm not a bird and not a cat, and I can think!" Li responds "That is your problem".

They practice the eye reap and sidekick in one. Making them one motion, not individual movements, one two, one two. just one...

The final scene with Bruce in this episode cuts to Li having Mike facedown on the floor and on top in a rear choke. Li teaches him to win at any cost. Mike has little clue about what to do, Li says "Bite!".

Spell Legacy Like Death - 21st October 1971 - Episode 6

This episode is about a dying man who plants bombs around the city. Mike suspects the bomber is someone from a past case and goes to confront the bomber to pay the ransom or is he?

Bruce is first shown as Li and Mike are training. Mike has progressed by this point. Li is circling Mike who can now track just by sound. Mike launches a kick directly at Li on target. Li just blocks and reaps his legs sending Mike right up into the air.

Mike gets a phone call from the bomber and has to leave. Li asks if he can tag along to see if he can help in any way, and Mike agrees and then takes Li as a "consultant" in the case.

In the next scene, at the Police station, where they are discussing the morality of paying the ransom of $500,000 (c.$3.5M in 2022) and if they do, opening the floodgates for anyone to make demands.

The evidence they have of the bomber is the recorded telephone calls. Conveniently utilising and enhancing Mike's Jeet Kune Do journey. As Mike is the "bagman", he must also learn how to defuse the bombs by touch alone. As they discuss clues they whittle down the suspects to down to a previous suspect from 1969, Lester Bailey. Mike gets ready and goes to confront him with his guide dog, Pax. They are in a sombre mood not quite expecting Mike to return. Li says "Maybe you'll be back in time to finish the lesson"

Li is next shown in the background performing hip throws, Mike is showing

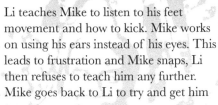

Li teaches Mike to listen to his feet movement and how to kick. Mike works on using his ears instead of his eyes. This leads to frustration and Mike snaps, Li then refuses to teach him any further. Mike goes back to Li to try and get him

back, and eventually, Li agrees. In the next scene, they are training and practising "sticky hands". Li tries to teach Mike the eye reap and Mike is uncomfortable with it; Li explains "The man who attacked you that night, would he hesitate to gauge out

Li's first appearance is bringing Nikki's antique sewing box to Mike who finds a secret compartment, that's empty. They discuss investigating this alone and Li is mainly in the background throughout these scenes. They go to the auction where the sewing machine was purchased. They essentially whittle the suspects down again to one man, Fred Decker.

They track down to where Nikki is held and go to rescue her... Next, Li appears and kicks the man holding Nikki. Nikki explains that Mike is being held by a knifeman in the building. When the knifeman is not looking Mike attacks and brawls with the man. Li finds them and the knifeman starts attacking Li, who holds him off with his kicks and then attacks with a flying kick taking down the knifeman.

The episode closes where they are joking about the value of the sewing machine now and cooking barbeque food.

"'I see', Said the Blind Man" - 18th November 1971 - Episode 10

Pax is critically stabbed whilst trying to stop a murder and when Mike turns up, realising that Mike is blind, the attacker just walks away into the night.

Li appears in the training scene at the start where he is doing bag work with Mike. Mike and Li are training in the background whilst the Police are asking about the case. They approach Mike who is feeling inadequate with his blindness and does not want to work on the case. He

progression as he uses his legs to catch Li in an ankle lock talking Li to the floor, and just sparring and having fun.

Wednesday's Child - 11th November 1971 - Episode 9

One of the reoccurring Police officers in this series, Nikki (Marlyn Mason) is kidnapped after purchasing an antique sewing machine and then held for ransom. Mike investigates with Li's help to discover what makes the machine so valuable and to find a way to rescue Nikki.

gets more aggressive with the bag and Li tells him it's time to quit.

In the last scene, the Police officer and Li are asked by Mike whether they are going to keep following him like his bodyguards. Li says "As long as you remain stubborn"

That was the last Bruce Lee was in Longstreet.

Summary

Longstreet promotes Bruce Lee's philosophy and the theories of Jeet Kune Do. This showcases Bruce's acting ability not just his moves. If you are expecting high-octane action, you may be disappointed. You do see however his signature stances and movements. It is definitely worth watching Bruce's episodes, especially the first and sixth episodes, but the show was also pretty good as well.

It is a shame he could not star in further episodes but Golden Harvest was waiting. The show contains many of Bruce's philosophies intertwined within the script and Bruce even says "that one". So, be water, my friends.

独占・誌上公開！★★★★★★★★「ロングストリート」の世界

ブルース★リー未発表
コレクションⅡ

幻のＴＶ映画
「ロングストリート」を
世界ではじめて
誌上公開した６月号が
大好評！　で、今月お贈
りするのはこれだ！

BRUCE LEE
IN LONGSTREET

嵐の前の沈黙
激闘のあとの静けさ

先日、ノラ・ミャオのお兄さんが来日した。彼の友人・温氏はカメラマンであり、鑑相家でもある。つまり手相を見る。温氏は生前のブルース・リーの手相を見ている。ブルース・リーの生命線は、驚くべきことに、普通の人の半分しかなかった！　という話を聞いた。突然の死は、やはり運命であった…しかし、彼の業績を讃え、武道家に贈られる最高の栄誉BRUCE　LEE　AWARDが設立され、先日、ロスで第1回トーナメントが行なわれた

（ここでは「ロングストリート」より、彼の表情を集めました。）

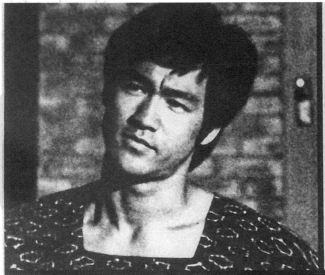

分解写真でとらえた
後まわし蹴り——

ブルース・リーの、技の早さについて解説するのは、やめよう。なぜなら、その恐るべき早さは、あなた自身が、いちばんよく知っているからだ。後まわし蹴りの早さについても、もはや言うまでもない。彼にしては比較的ゆるやかなこの「ロングストリート」中のシーンですら、分解写真でとらえようとすれば、ご覧のとおりだ。カメラが趣味だったブルース・リー……鏡の部屋で練習に励んだブルース・リー……彼の日常の行動のすべてが、武道を芸術に高めた、という事実にあらためて敬服するのである。

PHOTO／パラマウント・テレビジョン提供

BRUCE LEE THE GENTLE DRAGON STILL ALIVE IN YOUR HEART!

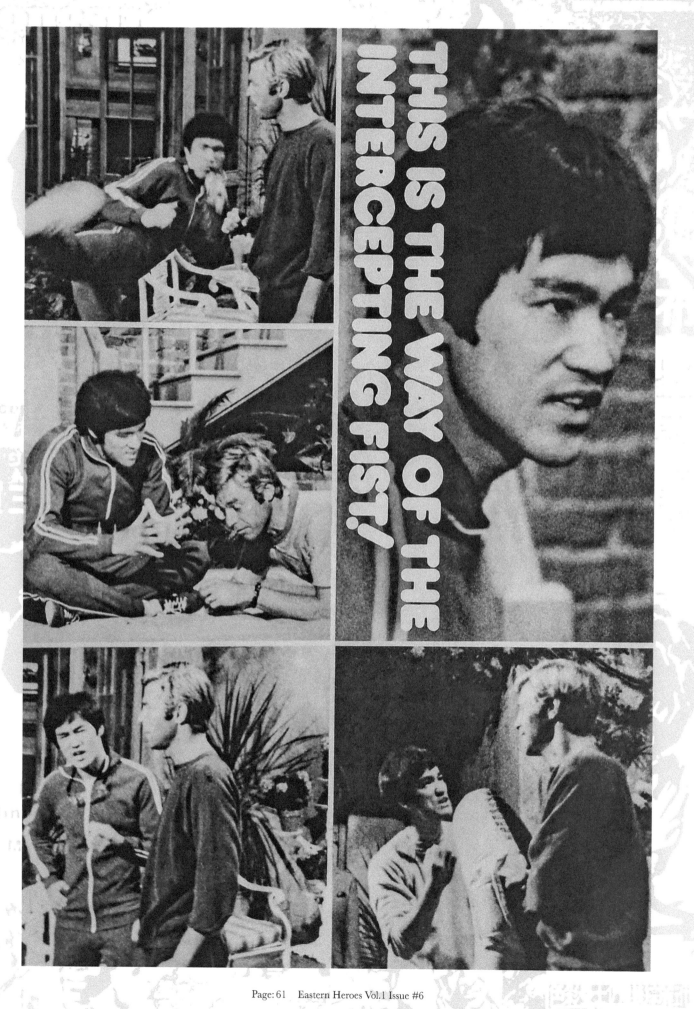

THIS IS THE WAY OF THE INTERCEPTING FIST!

THE BOSTON CONNECTION

By Alan Canvan

In the Fall of 1969, Bruce Lee was eagerly anticipating the release of his first American motion picture, Marlowe, which he'd filmed for MGM Studios roughly a year prior. The movie, a loose adaptation of Raymond Chandler's best selling novel The Little Sister, starred James Garner in the leading role. Lee's character, Winslow Wong, was specifically created for the feature by screenwriter Stirling Silliphant, Lee's devout Jeet Kune Do student and most vocal cheerleader in Hollywood, for the sole purpose of showcasing his martial guru's talents and keeping his flame alive in Tinsel Town. Lee's acting career had stalled following the cancellation of The Green Hornet TV series, and Silliphant convinced director Paul Bogart that Wong's character would be a fresh take on the mob enforcer archetype found in most crime noirs. Despite it being a relatively minor role with less than five minutes of screen time, Lee was elated at scoring his first American movie gig and intent on making it as dynamic as possible. To help promote the film, the studio sent him on a promotional tour to various martial art schools across the country. It was this endeavor that led him to George Mattson's Academy of Karate in Boston, Massachusetts.

Lee's acquaintanceship with Mattson dated back to the initial World Karate Tournament held in Chicago on July 28th, 1963. Mattson, who is acknowledged for bringing the Okinawan art of Uechi-ryu Karate to America, began his martial studies in the mid 1950's while stationed with the US Army in Okinawa. During that time, he met Ryuku Tomoyose and Kanei Uechi, whose father, Kanbun, had founded the art of Uechi-ryu following years of training with Shushiwa, a Chinese Monk and Tea Merchant who taught a southern Chinese art known as Pongainoon (which translates to 'half hard, half soft'). Mattson trained under Ryuku for several years, and promised his Sensei that he would promote the art in the United States. He returned home in 1958, began teaching at the YMCA in Boston, and eventually opened his own school - the Mattson Academy of Karate. Of Mattson's direct students, several would go on to make a name for themselves in the karate tournament circuit of the 1960's, including Bob Campbell, Jim Maloney and Art Rabesa.

"I first met Bruce in Chicago at the first major karate tournament held there," says George Mattson who was a tournament official." I believe in 1963. I also met him in California at the first Long Beach tournament and he was very aware of the style I taught. He was so small … you have to understand he was a nobody [then]. But he was somebody Ed Parker kept saying, 'You have to meet this guy'. Much has been written about his speed and skill, which I agree with based on what I saw during his demonstrations at the two tournaments."

As fate would have it, Lee reached out to Mattson six years later. "Essentially, Bruce came to my dojo when his new movie was released and I invited some of my senior students to come so they could get pictures with him and Bruce could get publicity action shots." In fact, Lee had a secondary, and more personal reason, to travel nearly 3,000 miles: he was hip to Uechi-ryu's origins stemming from the Fujian province of China, the birthplace as his mother art, Wing Chun, and was curious to compare the two styles firsthand. At the time, Mattson's school was one of the few that was legitimately

and some of his elder students. Among them were Jim Maloney, Jack Summers and two Kenpo practitioners from Japan, Taka and Sada, who had migrated to the Uechi-ryu system and been training in Boston for several years. The dojo was situated on a second floor walk up and measured

recognized in the country. Lee, who in his early days would trek across town to a Seattle watering hole to have his favorite root beer soda served in a frosted mug, carried the same attitude towards selecting a martial institute to promote his movie. Similar to the way he recruited the top martial art champions of the day to study under him, he viewed Mattson's school and reputation, in part, as the 'frosting on the mug'.

On the cool Autumn afternoon of Monday, October 27, 1969, four days before Marlowe's premier, Lee, sporting a striped mock turtle neck and straight legged white cotton pants, arrived at Mattson's Academy located at 3 Hancock Street in downtown Boston. With him were a photographer and handler provided by MGM, and he was greeted at the school by Mattson

over 2,000 square feet - spacious, even by today's standard. The entrance of the main lobby held a large shoe rack that directly faced a soda machine. To the main floor's right was a stream of windows overlooking the city and a few hanging heavy bags, while the opposite side housed a make shift gym with dumbbells. Following the introductions, Lee walked barefoot across the hardwood floors and performed a series of speed and strength demonstrations, showcasing his signature two finger pushups and catapulting the heavy bags with his notable sidekick. He then asked Mattson for a volunteer to stage some action shots. For years, Lee had used this blueprint at many martial art institutions to prove his personal combative science's efficacy over what he referred to as 'the classical mess' - or lack of spontaneity and freedom that he perceived in most martial art styles.

Almost always, this resulted in making the participants look highly inept as he dominated them with his incredible speed, power and technique. That template would be harder to follow with Jim Maloney.

Hailing from Nova Scotia, Jim Maloney's ancestors are Mi'kmaq Indians, the original natives that occupied the region of Nova Scotia, Quebec and Maine. Maloney grew up in Canada, raised by an authoritative father who impressed fortitude and grit in him form a very young age. "I had my Shaolin Temple Discipline Training early," he laughs. Maloney developed an interest in Karate, relocated to Boston and wound up on Mattson's doorstep in 1963. Under Mattson's tutelage, he earned his black belt in 1967, and went on to become the undefeated New England Champion in free fighting and cement breaking competitions. "My teacher, Master George Mattson, took me in fresh off the Indian Reservation and showed me a new way of life," he says with reverence. Amongst his Uechi -ryu brothers, Maloney is viewed as a force of nature. To his rivals in the tournament circuit, Maloney was known for his extreme toughness and competitive streak. "I think the difference between someone like Maloney and many others, without being offensive, is that he is genetically programmed for war," says one of Mattson's highest ranked instructors. "There's something coiled inside Maloney that explodes with fury when least expected. He has got that Redskin's killer instinct behind his blinding speed. With Jimmy facing you, it is always 'a bad day at Little Rock'."

Given his martial prowess and propensity for combat, it's not surprising that Maloney jumped at the chance to participate in Lee's exhibition. "I was a big fan from watching The Green Hornet, as was everyone in the room, and we were all a little awestruck just by him being in our dojo" says Maloney. "I weighed around 152lbs at the time and Bruce was probably around 130lbs." For him, it was a genuinely thrilling opportunity to help "Kato" publicize his new movie. After posing for a few simulated action images, the two men progressed to concentrated movement. What transpired in the stream of motion that followed depends on who you ask. "It wasn't

a sparring match," stresses Mattson. "Bruce and Jim were creating movements of fighting for the purpose of a possible promotional purpose. . . promoting Bruce's movie. Jim is an exceptional fighter and was not demonstrating HIS ability with Bruce, but moving about, providing a good defensive posture for Bruce's techniques. None of these pictures were used in public promotional ads, to my knowledge and only became available after Bruce's death."

Over the years, one particular photo in which Maloney's lead hand seems to be parrying a fully extended kick by Lee, has been the source of some speculation - specifically, whether the moment was created for the shot or if the two men were in motion. "During his visit to my dojo, he demonstrated his kicks on our heavy bag and set up a promotional picture with Jim by throwing a kick at him. Following the photo, Bruce mentioned to me that the kick wasn't very good because his back was injured and it was very painful to kick," recounts Mattson. "Was there was an element of sparring in the movement? Jim is a remarkable martial artist, but any gossip stating that he was in a sparring match or that he was in danger of being hit by the kick would be false,". He adds: "No sane superstar/actor would take the chance of 1.) getting injured or more importantly, 2.) take a chance of injuring a fan in an accident. We see in the news, cases where a drunk superstar pushes a picture taker or while drunk

punches someone. Lawyers love these cases which are worth lots of money to the 'injured' party and of course the lawyers." A persuasive argument, though logic and instinct don't always align. Mattson's deputy instructor and second-in-command, who was not present that day, received a detailed synopsis from Maloney: "He asked to spar with a volunteer and Maloney stepped forward. Maloney's fighting speed in those days was phenomenal. Bruce only weighed 127 lbs back then. He had a hard time against Jim who would charge him behind a wauke (circular blocks) screen sweeping away his kicks. In this shot you can see Bruce Lee about to be taken down by

Maloney who swatted the kick with a wauke while moving in. The beauty of it is that Uechi has the 'straight blast' similar to Wing Chun, but with open chain palms out of seisan that are extremely effective for short stop and take downs. Bruce wasn't used to that." As for the remaining photos: "What you see Bruce doing is a moving exchange with Maloney...he was never able to get close to him. In any case, Bruce's kick in the photo is way off

target, roundhouse or hook. I doubt he'd have picked this photo to show how good of a fighter he was. The problem he was having with Jim was he could not get anywhere near as close as he had hoped. Not a diss on Bruce but a compliment on Jimmy. He (Lee) certainly was a good fighter...but so were many others... Maloney being one of them."

Maloney, however, insists that he and Lee had arranged the kicks in advance so that Maloney could avoid, parry and block

them accordingly. "We weren't sparring. I was there to help make him look good in the photos," says Maloney. " It was an exchange of techniques between myself and Bruce with me being the recipient of his amazing speed." Mattson's deputy coach, who confirmed the details of the event via phone with Maloney in 2009, offers a different perspective on what transpired than what Maloney has told others: "He said that the exchanges were many and Bruce used some of the photos for his book of the action shots. He said

Bruce was trying to close the distance on him with his fast kicks, but never could. That he had to take it easy when jamming him because Lee only weighed 127 lbs. And George was telling Jimmy 'Take it easy,' for fear he'd knock him to the floor. Jimmy did confirm he got his wauke under his side and round kicks several time in a jamming fashion, once jarring him off balance but holding him up so he would not fall. And this is not a knock on Lee or a style, just a conversation about the wonderful skills of two fighters. A simple

friendly sparring match exhibition with no one trying to really outshine the other. In fact Bruce was in awe of Maloney's skills and so he complimented him. Jimmy was a gentleman and never really slammed Bruce into the ground as he could very easily. Again none of this is a diss on Bruce Lee. He was phenomenal fighter, but so was a Maloney, Campbell and others

spawned by the Uechi system, a style that has the greatest center line protection of any style I ever witnessed in the bloody tournaments of the day."

These conflicting accounts lead to the sixty- four thousand dollar question: What really happened? Did Maloney turn out to be more skilled than Bruce

expected? Was Maloney genuinely able to jam Bruce's kicks? Or was it akin to situations that many talented martial artists experience who lightly spar - or play act at sparring - with both practitioners believing they got the better of the other? The answer may lie in the old aphorism 'facts should never stand in the way of truth.' It's clear that the two men moved around with each other. What's in question is how much of that movement was competitive, and, if so, did Maloney prove to be more of a challenge than Lee anticipated. Oftentimes, in a ballistic exchange, the lines blur between perception and reality. During combat, a martial practitioner not only faces his/her opponent but, also, their own personal bias. Simply put, the practice of ritualized violence requires a healthy dose of self confidence and for fighters that compete professionally (as opposed to those who strictly learn self preservation), this quality is significantly magnified. Relinquishing one's ego takes an acute level of self-awareness that few achieve, and what's often referred to as 'friendly sparring' could and should be more accurately described as a restraint in follow through. Consequently, fighters experience an enhanced sense of competition while sparring that they otherwise wouldn't in a life and death violent assault. Bruce Lee and Jim Maloney wouldn't be immune to this dynamic and it's not something either man would be eager to share outside of their inner circle. It's noteworthy that, at no point during the visit , did Lee take up the 'classical mess' with Mattson. "During his conversations with me, he did not discuss Uechi-ryu nor did he mention being "anti style" nor did he talk about Jeet Kune Do" says Mattson. Whether this topic was avoided due to Lee feeling that it would be counter productive to his end goal at Mattson's school, or the result of him being genuinely impressed by Maloney's skill is up for speculation, though it's plausible that both men took away something significant that day: Lee may have walked away slightly humbled (at least for the moment) and Maloney may have felt validated in holding his own against a TV super-hero. Alternatively, and more likely, Lee may have been fully secure in his skills and viewed whatever he was unable to pull off as a momentary hiccup that wouldn't have affected the outcome of the exchange if the moves had been 'for real'.

What did the rest of the Uechi clan think of the future God of Martial Art? The consensus seems to be that Lee was viewed as a Hollywood star with a Hollywood attitude, not a martial warrior who just happened to fall in the movie business. Implausible as it may seem, in 1969, Bruce

Lee was not viewed, either by his peers or the general public, as the face of martial arts. To them, he was a footnote - an actor who shined a small spotlight on the arts by playing the part of a masked adventurer's sidekick on TV for one season, and, to a lesser degree, a tutor to celebrities - none of whom they would consider to be genuinely tough guys. In a way, their stance really isn't surprising considering many martial artists of the day, who did not directly train with Lee, often wrote him off as cocky, arrogant and somewhat pampered. It's fair to say that a few people in Mattson's camp wouldn't have disagreed with that assessment. Additionally, the fact that he hadn't fought competitively, coupled with the knowledge that he came from a show biz family, only reinforced their opinion of him as middleclass tough, at best. Ironically, their beliefs were only strengthened when the kid students arrived at the dojo for their 4pm children's Karate class, absolutely thrilled to meet Kato from The Green Hornet. Bruce graciously took photos with the children and senior students, and, following his farewells, departed to an assured future of immortality on celluloid - not by virtue of Marlowe, but as a result of unforeseen events that would lead him back to Hong Kong, his life coming full circle.

As I write this, a popular TV series, Better Call Saul, has two characters debate the outcome of "who would win in a fight Bruce Lee or Muhammad Ali "? As each man argues their point, a third character interrupts them and asks if, in this hypothetical match up, Lee has a gun. He then states that it's the only way Lee could win. Irrespective of his opinion, he makes a valid point. The issue arises, inherently, when truth conflicts with the narrative we need to give our heroes. Indeed, by pitting those heroes against the most worthy of opponents, we cement their legacy. It's the chief reason why we ask: could Bruce Lee have beaten Joe Louis/ Lewis? Mike Tyson? Rickson Gracie? Batman? The Incredible Hulk? Bob Wall? The Great Wall? etc. The common denominator in nearly all those who ask the question is the unconscious application of the combat sport model to 'a fight'. While sparring is a useful exercise to train and develop certain attributes in sport

combat (ie distance, rhythm, timing), it should never be confused with training for violence outside of a controlled arena. The violence that's experienced in 'a fight' often happens with no preparation or warning and the skills developed in sparring rarely transfer in those encounters. That said, it's nearly impossible to provide an accurate answer to the question of who would win in "a fight" because the outcome of a fight, with no rules, is highly rooted in the scenario and psychological mindset, rather than in the physical skill set of those participating. Superlatives don't hold up in the real world, and 'somedays you're the windshield, some days you're the bug'. This goes for Bruce Lee, Jim Maloney, Muhammad Ali and every other being on the planet.

Today, George Mattson continues to teach Uechi-ryu on the East Coast and has also furthered its growth in other countries, including Canada and Bermuda. Jim Maloney represents the International Uechi Ryu Karate Federation in Canada and has become one of the most respected coaches in the North East, renowned for training and mentoring many of the full contact fighting champions in the region.

And Bruce Lee would posthumously become a global icon, revered by most of the world as the lynchpin of everything martial in the 20th Century.

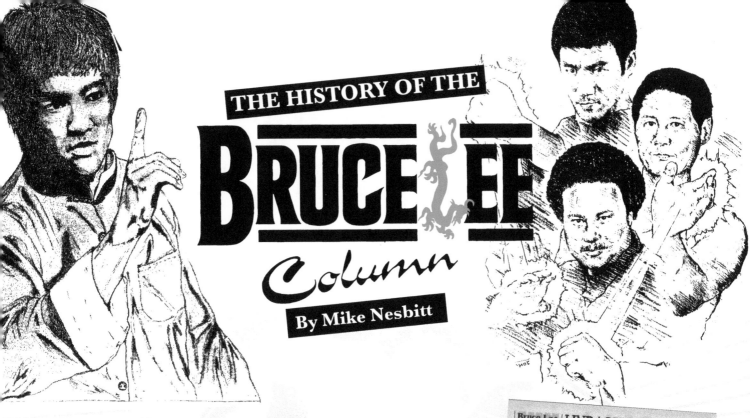

THE HISTORY OF THE BRUCE LEE Column

By Mike Nesbitt

What better way to start off the very first Bruce Lee Column than to pay tribute to the previous Bruce Lee Columns that have adorned the pages of various martial arts and movie magazines of the past? Strangely, apart from Kung Fu Monthly, which was a magazine solely dedicated to

Bruce Lee First came to the attention of Will Johnston in 1971 on Granada T.V.'s 'Cinema' review show during which they showed a clip from 'Big Boss' of Bruce leaping a fence whilst eating a bag of potato chips!!! It wasn't until January 1974 and the release of 'Enter the Dragon' that he seriously began to take an interest in Bruce Lee.

Becky Kimura and Andrew Staton at Bruce Lee's Grave in Seattle.

Bruce Lee, articles on Bruce Lee in martial arts and movie magazines in the UK during the 1970s, were very far and few between. One of the first instances where Bruce Lee had a cover article dedicated

to him, was in the International Times (IT) newspaper/magazine, dated the 11th of August 1973, less than a month after Bruce Lee's death. The only other time International Times featured Bruce, was in volume 2 number 1, released in March 1974. The first martial arts magazine to feature Bruce Lee with a cover article was Karate and Oriental Arts Magazine, which first featured him in March/April 1974 with issue number 47, Bruce would go on to have cover articles in at least another 8 issues throughout the 1970s, but this was by no means on a regular basis. One of the only other martial arts magazines that featured Bruce specifically with a cover article was Fighters Monthly, they pictured Bruce on the cover in its premier issue, and also on the cover of issue 3, both released in 1978. As for movie magazines, Bruce appeared in the October 1973 edition of Films and Filming, but it was only Film Review Magazine that featured Bruce Lee in multiple issues, starting with the July 1974 issue. Most of the other magazines that featured Bruce were usually one-shot issues or just regular issues that featured Bruce only once. Magazines such as; Bruce Lee: The King of Kung Fu, Legend of Bruce Lee, Look-In, Popster and Kung Fu, all released in 1974. During the 1980s Bruce didn't fare much better, only appearing sporadically in a few publications, including Music and Video Magazine

Issue 5. It wasn't until the late 1980s that magazines saw the benefit of having Bruce Lee in every issue and so began the golden age of The Bruce Lee Column.

MARTIAL ARTS ILLUSTRATED MAGAZINE

On Friday the 28th of July 1989, The Daily Sport newspaper ran a centre page spread about Bruce Lee. Andrew Staton, the man behind the Bruce Lee Association Fan Club, was also featured in it. This brought Andrew to the attention of the martial arts magazine, Martial Arts Illustrated. There were already rumours

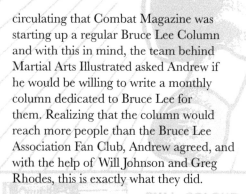

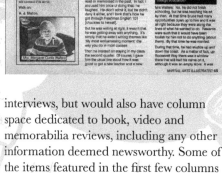

circulating that Combat Magazine was starting up a regular Bruce Lee Column and with this in mind, the team behind Martial Arts Illustrated asked Andrew if he would be willing to write a monthly column dedicated to Bruce Lee for them. Realizing that the column would reach more people than the Bruce Lee Association Fan Club, Andrew agreed, and with the help of Will Johnson and Greg Rhodes, this is exactly what they did.

The first column they wrote was called 'A Finger Pointing', which appeared in Vol 2 No 5, the October 1989 issue. The column was mainly focused on Bruce Lee's fighting style, and included fact files and

interviews, but would also have column space dedicated to book, video and memorabilia reviews, including any other information deemed newsworthy. Some of the items featured in the first few columns were as follows:

A Finger Pointing Column
Column 1 - An Introduction to the team, Andrew, Will and Greg. There was information on the Bruce Lee Memorial Day which would take place in October 1989, and a Chris Kent Biography.
Column 2 - Featured a JKD family Tree and the first of a series of fact files, No 1 being Bruce Lee. Also included was an interview with one of Bruce's top students,

Dan Inosanto. There was also a report on the Bruce Lee Memorial Day and a book review for Bruce Lee's Fighting Methods Volume 1: Self-Defense Techniques.
Column 3 - Had a transcription of a Bruce Lee audio interview; and two book reviews, the first being the new Linda Lee biography, The Bruce Lee Story, with the second book review being Bruce Lee's Fighting Methods Volume 2: Basic Training.
Column 4 - Started off with a Dan Inosanto video review; Fact File No 2 on Taky Kimura; and the AMA Interview with Larry Hartsell. There was also information on Jerry Poteet's England Seminar and the book review for Bruce

Bruce Lee in the

M E D I A

With the release of all the old *Kung Fu Monthlies* with this issue of M.A.I., some of you will realise that a lot of merchandise was produced over the years on Bruce Lee - some was good and some was bad. But one of the better projects was two audio tapes. One of these was called "Bruce Lee - The Last Interview"; of course it was not the last interview but it was a interview with Bruce and the transcript of this interview was printed in an earlier issue of M.A.I.

One of the more interesting interviews was on the rest of the tape and dealt with Linda Lee's tribute to Bruce Lee on Hong Kong radio, and also an interview with Linda at the Lee's Hong Kong home on Cumberland Road after Bruce Lee's death. For those of you who are so interested in what Linda Lee's life with Bruce was like this interview may give you the information you are looking for. As for Linda Lee's opinions today forget it, she is a private happily married individual and just gets on living her life and doesn't want to be pestered about the past.

LINDA LEE'S TRIBUTE TO BRUCE LEE

AND INTERVIEW ON HONG   KONG RADIO

73/74

LINDA LEE'S TRIBUTE TO BRUCE

Linda Lee: Since Bruce has past away in July I have have received many letters from people in Hong Kong who have not signed their names and who have not given their return address, and also I'm sure there are many other people who wanted to communicate their feeling to me, because so many people loved Bruce. I'd like to thank all those people. It has been a great help for me to know I have many friends here, even though I'm not Chinese and you have welcomed me into your city and into you hearts.

Interviewer: Linda, do you take personal interest in these letters and if you had the chance to reply, would you?

Linda Lee: Yes, I have replied to some of them, in fact I will reply to all of the ones that I can. It's just with all this inquest going on and everything I have a lot of things to do. While I'm here I may not get the replies done as soon as I should, but I will reply to the ones that I can.

Interviewer: Linda Lee, thank you very much.

Linda Lee: Your welcome.

LINDA LEE'S INTERVIEW AT THE LEE'S HOME IN HONG KONG

The interview starts with the interviewer asking Linda what connection Sam and Reebo Hoi had with the Lee family.

Linda Lee: Sam and Reebo Hoi have been my very close friends for quite a while but sine Bruce passed away they have given me so much help and support and friendship without asking for anything in return. I don't think that I could have been as strong as I have been or tried to have been without their support and friendship.

Interviewer: I heard from Reebo that your association with them was quite by accident. Is that right, about how you met?

Linda Lee: Well, they came back to Hong Kong at about the same time as we did, and we were all taken to dinner by the Golden Harvest people. With Becky and I not being so keen on the different kinds of Chinese food - we were eating ducks tongue and eel and things like that - on one particular night we were glancing at each other across the table and chuckling, and I guess maybe because we were both Americans and come from similar backgrounds we struck up a very close friendship.

BRUCE and BRANDON LEE
in the media

Well, Way of the Dragon hit the TV screens recently - and was totally uncut, apart from the nunchakus and one other scene!

All I can say is it was a mixed blessing, and Will Johnston has a fuller report this month. New Bruce Lee merchandise is currently on its way from Media Asia, and to back this we have a colour *Way of the Dragon* souvenir brochure in November's issue of our sister publication, *Impact*.

We have some great footage of Brandon scheduled for our convention on November 30th at Pictureville, so be there and don't miss this great event.

Watch this space for a full update on Bruce and Brandon, and watch out for Bruce's daughter Shannon who is making it big in films. We will have a full report soon.

May it be well with you.

A.J. Staton.

After twenty-five years' wait, Bruce Lee's much acclaimed film *Way of the Dragon* was shown for the first time on Channel Four in the early hours of Saturday, 20th of September.

The version shown was in widescreen format and its original Chinese language, unfortunately many fans will still have been sorely disappointed that the long-awaited insertion of the 'double nun-chaku' scene did not materialise. This is a shame as the first fight scene in the movie did not appear until 1.20am, hardly a threat to the watershed time of 9pm. What was gratifying was that the remaining fight scenes, with the exception of the gunman in Miss Chen's apartment (the section where Bruce 'claws' his face), were shown fully uncut, which itself says more about unnecessary editing of the Rank copies than at first obvious.

Think about it, the TV company went through the film looking for any offensive footage and in the process *ignored* five fight scenes, which in the Rank version are decimate, if it wasn't so annoying it would be laughable.

Many people have commented that they enjoyed this original Chinese version of *Way of the Dragon* even more than its dubbed version. This in probably because it's precisely is this format that Bruce intended it to be shown; he had no intention of releasing it overseas with an 'added' English sound track. Most of the in-jokes, such as the misunderstanding over the menu and receiving Campbells soup instead of eggs, make perfect sense when we hear Bruce grappling with a foreign language, trying to say 'eggs' in English but failing miserably. On the English dub Bruce appears to say 'eggs' perfectly well, yet is still misunderstood by the Italian waitress... this is probably why most of these scenes are missing from the U.S. prints of the film. It just doesn't make sense if the soundtrack is all dubbed into English. Anyway if anyone had their video recorder working this night they won't have been disappointed.

Though it's a shame that Polygram are selling *Way of the Dragon* at the budget price of £5.99, since it is more cut than the TV version, still it's selling very well. If only they had got an original print from Hong Kong and remastered the film widescreen and uncut.

Full report on *Big Boss* and *Game of Death* when they have been screened on Channel Four at 12.35am on Friday 10th and 17th of October respectively.

WAY OF THE DRAGON on TV

By Will Johnston and A.J. Staton

COVER STORY

Lee's Fighting Methods Volume 3: Skill in Techniques.

Column 5 - Had a Chuck Norris interview; Fact File No 3, which focused on Dan Inosanto and the book review for Bruce Lee's Fighting Methods Volume 4: Advanced Techniques.

By 1991, it was decided by the Martial Arts Illustrated team, to feature two regular columns dedicated to Bruce Lee every month. There was already The Finger Pointing Column, which would now solely be on Bruce Lee's fighting arts. And instead of the 'Bruce Lee in the Media' section being in the Finger Pointing Column, it would become its own column, focusing on everything else relating to Bruce. The first Bruce Lee in the Media Column appeared in Vol 4 No 9 issue of Martial Arts Illustrated, dated February 1992. Some of the first columns included information on Chuck Norris's book, The Secret of Inner Strength; Brandon Lee in the TV and movie O'Hara and Kung Fu; Those Who Died Young book review; and the Bruce Lee Association. Some of the early articles also included:

Bruce Lee in the Media Column
Column 1 - The Secret of Inner Strength; Kung Fu The Movie; Brandon Lee in O'Hara; The Incredibly Strange Jonathan Ross Rides Again; TV Dragon Roles On; Book review - Those Who Died Young; and the Bruce Lee Association.

Column 2 - Green Hornet Stings the Comic Scene; Best of Martial Arts on Sell-Through; Bruce Lee T-Shirts in the Transfer; Kung Fu Monthly Alive and Kicking.

Column 3 - Plenty of Dragons but No Tracking; Brandon Joins Rocky's Russian Opponent; Bruce Lee Spoof in Police Academy 2; End of the Year Shows Enter the Dragon.

Column 4 - Ironside: Tagged for Murder, review of the TV episode featuring Bruce Lee.

Column 5 - Linda Lee's Tribute to Bruce Lee, transcription of an old audio

A FINGER POINTING

I always find it interesting when someone tries to compare Jeet Kune Do to new martial arts styles, or compare one instructor to another. I had a comment a few weeks ago from a kick-boxer who said: "Well, I've seen a J.K.D. instructor, and I don't think he would last two seconds in a street fight". In some ways I can see what he is saying, on the other hand every street fight is different. In J.K.D.'s defence it is a method that leads to individuality, and if the individual does not train sufficiently then of course J.K.D. will be analysed badly.

In an attempt to help these poor mis-informed individuals, this month we are printing two articles by Cass Magda, one is called "How Bruce Lee is being mis-interpreted" and the other is "When in doubt, straight blast". I hope these articles help clear things up; if not, write in and let us know *your* views.

J.K.D. for now.

A. J. Staton.

> "Absorb what is useful. Reject what is useless. Add what is specifically your own. Man, the creating individual is more important than any established style or system"
> *Bruce Lee.*

HOW BRUCE LEE IS BEING MIS-INTERPRETED

By Cass Magda

Cass Magda.

The philosophy of Jeet Kune Do has inspired many martial artists to a more investigative and open approach to learning and training, as well as inspiring the current wave of eclectism in the martial arts. Everyone these days is "using what works". New eclectic styles preaching "totality" and "freedom of expression" are sprouting up everywhere.

Sadly, these new styles are nothing but a reaction; new packages of reorganised despair claiming similarity to J.K.D. in their philosophy and application, but in fact by doing this they are missing the idea. My point here is not to argue over what is original (because nothing is really original), who had what first or who is borrowing from whom. These issues are unimportant. The philosophy of J.K.D. is like any other philosophy, people can add or express their own interpretation of it. What Bruce Lee meant by the J.K.D. philosophy in practical application is sometimes a far

cry from those martial artists claiming to follow it. One of the most commonly mis-interpreted phrases is the "Absorb what is useful" saying that opened this discussion.

The idea of absorbing what is useful does not mean choosing, collecting, compiling, accumulating or assembling techniques from different styles of martial arts, thinking to yourself, "I'll take the best from all the styles and put it together to form a new style". To do this is to miss the point. We are not saying "collect what you like" or "put together the best" but absorb what is useful. It is an individual investigation. To 'absorb' means to 'get into' the technique/training method you are interested in until you develop a 'feel' for it. Until you experience 'being' in it and becoming it you don't really understand it. For example, looking at the Malaysian art of Bersilat, trying out a few of their techniques, then saying to yourself, "I like their elbow technique, I think I'll add it to my style" is a step into the mud hole of self-delusion. To understand

Bruce shows student Dan Lee the advantages of taking control of the centre.

those techniques you need to go into the Malaysian art and train like they do, feel it, experience it for a while, both in the doing and the receiving, until you've got a grasp on it. You must become a Bersilat man in order to truly understand Bersilat techniques, attitudes, training methods, etc. Once you have 'absorbed it', that experience and knowledge gained is yours, not just interview with Linda. Future issues featured Interviews with the likes of Bruce Lee's Teacher, Margaret Walters, Linda Lee, Brandon Lee, James Coburn, Louis Lin, and Shannon Lee, among many others. There were also articles on Bruce Lee's life and death, his movies, TV shows, conventions and memorabilia reviews, which included books, magazines, videos, comics, and records. After Brandon Lee died in 1993, the column had a name change to the Bruce and Brandon Lee in the Media, and would focus both on father and son. The Martial Arts Illustrated Bruce Lee Column would end up becoming the longest-running Bruce Lee Column in the World.

COMBAT MARTIAL ARTS MAGAZINE

Both Martial Arts Illustrated and Combat Martial Arts Magazines were fighting to become the first magazine to feature a regular Bruce Lee Column, but they ended up sharing that privilege, as Combat, just like Martial Arts Illustrated, released their first Bruce Lee Column in October 1989. However, unlike Martial Arts Illustrated which released its premiere issue in June 1988, Combat had featured Bruce Lee in their magazine several times since its first issue in September 1974. Weirdly, even though Bruce Lee appeared on the front cover of the first issue, there was no Bruce Lee related article within its pages, but he did go on to have at least five other cover articles in future issues, before the Bruce Lee Columns foundation. In Combat's very first Bruce Lee Column, in Volume 15 Number 11 of Combat, an article written by Bey Logan, who would incidentally write most of the forthcoming columns, talked about the now infamous Steve Cattle vs Bruce Lee argument. Steve had stated in his own monthly column that Bruce Lee would have been no match for the likes of Dolph Lundgren and Steve Morris. This caused a huge uproar within the Bruce Lee and Martial Arts communities. With one side saying Bruce would easily win both and the other side saying he wouldn't. The Second column was written by Bruce Lee student, Larry Hartsell, and even featured a rare photo of Bruce and Larry together. The following three Bruce Lee Columns, written by Bey Logan, were a three-part article on the search for the real Game of Death story and footage. Even though Bey would write

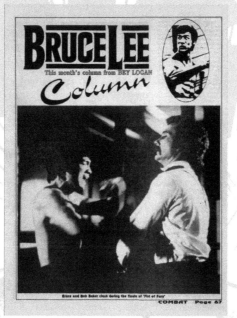

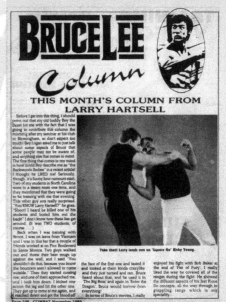

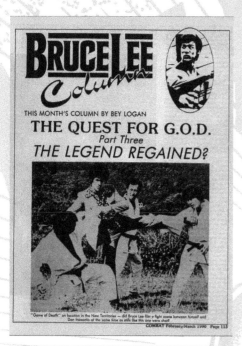

BRUCE LEE Column

This month's column by BEY LOGAN

THE QUEST FOR G.O.D.
Part Three
THE LEGEND REGAINED?

"Game of Death" on location in the New Territories — did Bruce Lee film a fight scene between himself and Dan Inosanto at the same time or stills like this one years shelf?

COMBAT February/March 1990 Page 113

BRUCE LEE Column

This month's column by BEY LOGAN

Don't look now, Bruce, but Bolo could be putting in an appearance at your fifteenth birthday party, which will be staged in England to launch a new book series.

Page 120 COMBAT April 1990

BRUCE LEE Column

YOU'RE ONLY FILMED TWICE

BEY LOGAN EXAMINES 'DR.NO' AND FINDS OUT WHY 'ENTER THE DRAGON' HAS BEEN CALLED 'THE GREATEST JAMES BOND FILM NEVER MADE'.

Ian Fleming, creator of James Bond 007, and author of 'Dr.No', the basis for 'Enter the Dragon'.

Page 96 COMBAT May 1990

BRUCE LEE Column

This month's column by MARK HOUGHTON

RETURN OF THE (FAT) DRAGON!
: SAMO HUNG PLAYS TRIBUTE TO BRUCE!

Stars Samo Hung and Karl Heke go to bat in 'Skinny Tiger, Fatty Dragon'.

Page 52 COMBAT July 1990

BRUCE LEE Column

By GEORGE TAN

THE MAKING OF "FIST OF FURY"

Page 72 COMBAT December 1990

BRUCE LEE Column

IN HONOUR OF BRUCE LEE!
TRACKING THE DRAGON '90 — CONVENTION REPORT
By MARC STOREY

Left to right: Will Johnston, Bob Baker, John Saxon, Howard Williams, George Tan. Hosting The "Tracking The Dragon" convention.

Page 40 COMBAT March 1991

BRUCE LEE Column

COLLECTING BRUCE LEE MEMORABILIA
SECTION 1 BY CHRIS ALEXIS
TAKING A PIECE OF THE "LITTLE DRAGON HOME"

Bruce disposing of Chan Loong.

COMBAT April 1991 Page 82

BRUCE LEE Column

By GEORGE TAN

AN INTERVIEW WITH THE DRAGON

Page 58 COMBAT June 1992

BRUCE LEE Column

BY SHAUNE BRIDGWOOD

"WHO WAS BRUCE LEE?"

Bruce Lee, possibly the God Father of Martial Arts, universally.

BRUCE LEE Column

Apart from Bruce Lee himself, when one hears the term JEET KUNE DO, it is instantly associated with names who have become immediately recognisable over the years. Generally referred to as the 'JKD Clan', these people have been talked about, written about, interviewed and seminared frequently the world over. It is therefore quite refreshing to hear of someone new who can genuinely be acredited the title of a *true* JKD man. He began training with Bruce Lee and James Lee in Oakland, California at the tender age of 15, the youngest of their students ever, having no prior knowledge of any fighting skills. I'm speaking off course of Mr Howard Williams.'

To many of the loyal readers of Combat, the name 'Howard Williams' has only been associated with the late great Bruce Lee in recent months, when he made his first visit to these shores to attend the now historic 'Tracking the Dragon' Convention in December last year to celebrate what would have been Bruce's 50th Birthday. This interview was conducted by Chris Alexis of Martial Club, the organisor of the aforementioned event just a few days after its conclusion. Before proceeding with a review of this tape, I would like to make it clear that although it is a Video Interview I do not feel it appropriate to disect it on a word for word basis. To do this would be to lose all the 'emotional content'. Indeed what this gentleman has to say to some very probing questions will have everyone sitting up, from the youngest fan to the oldest martial artist and especially existing JKD practitioners. So a general overview of the tape will be given.

The majority of this video centres around Howard's views and opinions of the current JKD scene as well as his own personal roots and roots in the Art together with his quite vivid recollections of the learning experiences with Bruce Lee and James Lee.

Howard grew up in the Oakland area which in his own words was the rough part of Oakland. You had to be able to look after yourself. His childhoo couldn't be described as being settled. In fact Howard reveals that he had to run away from home and live with his Stepfather in order to learn Gung-Fu. It was his stepfather who went out looking for a school that Howard could attend. This in itself was not particularly easy, especially given that the Orientals at that time were not happy to share their martial arts knowledge with Westerners. Howard's stepfather however got lucky. He literally ran into

Bruce one day outside the school just as Bruce was putting a sign up. Howard then came and met Bruce who in turn introduced him to James Lee and began training at the age of 15.

The beginning of the training was an event in itself because as Howard reveals he was thrown into the advanced class and told by James "Don't worry, you'll catch on quickly". This he certainly did.

A bit further on into the Video-Interview, Howard reveals some amusing anecdotes about training with Bruce and James which I won't reveal in these pages lest it spoil your anticipated enjoyment. I will tell you that Bruce had a nickname for Howard. "Bruce called me RUGGED", he he used to say "He's Rugged", Howard reveals. Sometime later, James Lee's son Greg Lee told Howard that he had overheard Bruce and James discussing him several times and James praising his development and Bruce commenting that he's got natural speed and power, like naturally athleticc. Bruce told James that he had had to work harder to get to the speed and power which at that point Howard had achieved. Praise indeed!! Howard gives several further examples of incidents which took place to illustrate this. You'll have to see the video for yourselves to find out all. All of this and more stories of 'hanging out' socially with Bruce & James and with their respective families. Howard speaks of these times with warmth and a large slice of affection.

Asked whether JKD as it is taught today is how Bruce intended it to be, Howard replies with an intense and very definite No, No, No, NO!!! He continues on, saying that it does not resemble in the slightest anything similar to what Bruce was trying to get his students in the 1st generation to learn!!!!!

Naturally enough this is where this 90 minute (approx) interview begins to get interesting. "It's like having a fine wine that has been watered down so that it has the colouring but the flavour is missing." No doubt such a statement will be considered in some quarters to be offending. Some may consider this an attention grabbing attempt for the purposes of self promotion. Perhaps he's bluffing or perhaps he's just got a lot of guts!!!??? Are these opinions just meant to be thought provoking? 'Probably'. But more importantly can he back them up? ANd that's not all. Howard goes even further to state that had Bruce Lee been alive he would not approve of what is being taught today as it misses the essence of what Bruce was trying to get across.

"He in fact would probably be so disturbed by the whole thing that he would probably shut everything down"! Within this interview, Howard clearly wants it understood that he has not gone public before as he was never after the glory of having his name linked with that of Bruce Lee especially for commercial reasons. "I was kind of coached into coming out now after all these years, and then I had to rethink about it to find reasons within myself for why I wanted to come out. I was going to carry on and go ahead to be content with keeping the art to myself. I knew how to fight. It's their problem if they didn't. I was being sort of selfish about it". The more I heard of the CANCEROUS DISEASE that was being taught and spread, the more it got to me the more angry I became, and sometimes I could hardly WAIT to get out there and tell of what real JKD is about. Howard credits the people who persuaded him to go the public as being Bob Baker, Ted Wong and Jerry Poteet.

It is not for me to use these pages to go into an indepth analysis of these comments, nevertheless I can tell you that Howard himself continues with this in mind and it is compelling viewing.

There are many clues to Howard's character within this Video-Interview. His persona comes across very well. It is the persona of a gentleman who is extremely self-assured yet instantly likeable. His calm and relaxed exterior manner belies the ferocious and aggressive fighting abilities that lie beneath the surface and God help anyone who dares to trifle with the man. There is a definite sense of sincerity in what he says combined with an intense passion. This I believe comes from an immeasurable loyalty which is easy to see, towards Bruce and James which translates itself in the manner he puts his views and opinions across. It's just the way he tells it. You don't get the feeling that he is deliberately trying to put anyone down and neither is he paying lip-service to anybody. He is simply saying what needs to be said. After all TRUTH IS TRUTH. His personality itself becomes subject to discussion when the observation is made that he can come across as being 'Cocky', a trait that is identified quite strongly with Bruce by virtually everyone who knew him. With a wry smile and a chuckle, Howard replies that it is really being confident about yourself and your abilities. It is about finding out who you really are by determining the 'cause of your ignorace' and then being able to have

THE WAY OF THE INTERCEPTING FIST

by HOWARD WILLIAMS

the willingness to do something about it eventually leading to the TRUTH. So as far as Howard is concerned it is not being cocky, it's being confident.

Howard also states that he can become more powerful and faster than he already is. On a personal note I can't wait to see this although I'm not entirely sure that I would like to experience it first hand. When Howard was over her he did manage to get in a brief demonstration and seminar at the events he attended and one or two people were able to experience the power and speed he has at his command first hand. AGain you will be able to hear for your self as Howard relates what happened at these demos. Many are already calling the closest thing to Bruce Lee that ever lived in terms of his his JKD. The ending of theis video should be closely watched as all I will say is that it is EXPLOSIVE. For those of you wishing to aquire Bruce-like skills you have a supreme example and the opportunity. Martial Club will be bringing Howard back to England later this year for a series of seminars and details will be announced soon. DON'T MISS IT.

In the meantime the video is highly recommended to every and anybody with an interest in Bruce Lee. In fact you will probably need to watch it a few times. Once to enjoy Howard's personality. Once again to take in the content of what he's saying, and the next time to put it all together and LEARN. It would certainlly be advisable especially if like me you are looking forward to training with Howard. If the physical side of things is not your cup of tea, the video will either make you want to train or you will be able to enjoy the many aspects and stories of Bruce's most developing years. As for the ending, "**ff??/()¡!!!&£$" is what you'll be saying. It is available at a cost of £20.00 + £2.00 p&p from Martial Club at P.O. Box 445, Lavendar Hill, Battersea, London, SW11. Telephone (071) 738 2506. Incidentally, we understand that some of you have written to Howard after his address was published in these pages a few months ago. Please be patient for a reply as he trains quite vigorously, up to six hour day. It would also help if you enclosed an international reply coupon available from the Post Office. In the meantime, Happy Viewing.

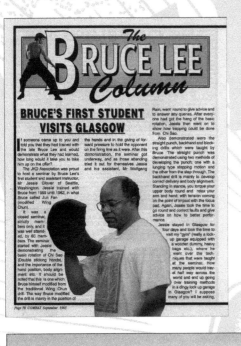

BRUCE LEE Column

SHEK KIN ('HAN' OF "ENTER THE DRAGON")

AND BRUCE LEE (LEI SIU LOONG)

BY VICTOR I.T. APPIAH

In 1985, while Victor Appiah was on the film set of Jackie Chan's "Police Story" with his friend, Mars, he received a phone call from Shaw Brothers Film Company. The man who called him was another old friend, martial artist, actor and director Wong Lung Wai (known to all his fans in England as 'THE MAYOR'). He has starred in tens of Martial Arts films, his most memorable ones are "Martial Club", "Young Auntie" and "The Lady Is Boss". He told Victor that Mr Shek Kin ('Han' of 'Enter the Dragon' fame) had heard of him and wanted to meet him as he wanted Victor to star alongside him in a film he was making: "Heroes of Tsim Sha Tsui East" (Jihm Dung Hieu Hung). Victor could not believe his luck as this was the big break that he had been waiting for. He took a taxi straight away and went to Shaw Brothers Company to meet the big man, Shek Kin, himself. They had lunch together. Shek Kin told Victor that he had heard of him, because director Wong Lung Wai had told him on several occasions that he knew a black guy who spoke fluent Cantonese. Shek Kin said he did not believe the director and wanted to meet Victor and hear his accent for himself. Victor was given a big part and starred alongside Shek Kin. As the weeks past, Victor got very close to Shek Kin and they talked about many things.

Victor says that he believes that not many people who have seen "Enter The Dragon" would believe that the man who fought Bruce Lee was already a pensioner in his 60s! His vitality comes from training in 'real' Kung Fu. Shek Kin is a Kung Fu man first, an actor second.

Although Shek Kin was in his 70's in 1985, during the fight scenes his hands and feet were still so fast it was unbelievable! For a man of his age he was very nible. And like all true Martial Artists he was a real gentleman - courteous and polite.

He answered every question that Victor put to him. He said that he's been in the film industry for more than 40 years and that nine out of ten times he had played the villain, as in "Enter The Dragon" and that over the years he had, on screen, died a thousand deaths in all manner of ways, from being shot or knifed, to falling from a high cliff to a watery grave.

Shek Kin, who is known to his friends and admirers as 'Kin Suk' - the Can-

COMBAT August 1993 Page 71

---

many of the articles, future columns would be written by the likes of Mark Houghton, George Tan, Chris Alexis, Mark Storey, Malcolm Martin and many others. Articles included:

The Bruce Lee Column

Column 1 - The Bruce Lee v Dolph Lundgren debate written by Bey Logan.
Column 2 - Article written by Bruce lee student Larry Hartsell.
Column 3-5 - A 3-part article on the lost story and footage of Game of Death by Bey Logan.
Column 6 - The George Tan ten-book series update by Bey Logan.
Column 7 - The comparison between James Bonds Dr No and Enter the Dragon by Bey Logan.
Column 8 - On the set of Skinny Tiger, Fatty Dragon by Mark Houghton.
Columns 9-12 - Game of Death – An Analysis in four parts by David G. Hall.
Column 13 - The Making of Fist of Fury by George Tan.
Column 14 - The Making of the Big Boss by Chris Alexis.
Column 15 - Tracking the Dragon Convention 1990 by Marc Storey.

By Volume 22 No 7, dated July 1996, the monthly writing of the column was taken over by Chris Ducker, who had just formed the Bruce Lee Fan Club, The Bruce Lee Pen Pal Society. What makes this Bruce Lee Column extra special for me, is that my name appeared for the first time in print in Volume 22 No 12, dated December 1996, in a Bruce Lee article written by Chris, called Tao of the Dragon Warrior.

The Bruce Lee Column

The Bruce Lee Column

Bey Logan presents a monthly round-up of fresh information on The Little Dragon.

Why Now?

After all these years, surely the idea of a column devoted to the late, great Bruce is truly passe? Why would anyone but a die hard member of the Geek Kune Do fraternity consider such a thing? My reasons for instituting this monthly round-up of Leedom are threefold: Firstly, there seems no evidence whatsoever that the world's fascination with The Little Dragon has diminished. In fact, there seems to be even MORE interest, as a whole new generation of fans discover the man's life and work. Secondly, I feel I still owe something to Lee for his contribution to my own life, as both a writer and a martial artist, and this column seems an obvious way to keep the flame. Finally, I've realised that there really is a lot of Bruce Lee information that has still yet to be disseminated, and especially material from sources in the Far East. I'm sure the Impact readership will show no hesitation in telling me what they think of this retroactive action, but, for now, anyway, Bruce Lee lives! (And so does Elvis...)

THE SUPER 8 ARCHIVES : FURTHER LOST FOOTAGE

Think you've seen it all? Think again. We've come across at least three individuals who allegedly shot Super 8 footage of Bruce, though their footage has yet to be released. The best-known of these is *Enter the Dragon* co-star Ahna Capri who, according to long-time fan Toby Russell, shot behind-the-scenes footage on the set of *Enter*, including (get this!) Bruce teaching Bolo to cha-cha. We'd pay big money to see that, and that's exactly what Ms Capri is looking for. Toby says she had the film valued by Sotherbys, and that's why it didn't appear on *Death by Misadventure*. Our own Bey The Beast has been trying, in vain, so far, to track down Peter 'Do I bother vit?' Archer, using his unique contacts in Hong Kong and Australia. According to Bey's step-father, and Archer's former friend, Tino Ceberano, Peter returned from shooting *Enter the Dragon* with both still photos and Super 8 footage of the experience. Archer was an Australian businessman and Shotokan karate black belt living in Hong Kong at the time *Enter* was made. If he's reading this, Peter, please call Tino or Bey, both of whom are in the phone book! Finally, there's the case of the *Way of the Dragon* crew-member who shot behind-the-scenes Super 8 footage on the set of that film. Hong Kong radio personality, and long-time Lee fan, Lot Sze tells of how this fellow made the

Bruce Lee during a press interview on the Fist Of Fury set.

mistake of lending his footage to someone else and then... You've guessed it! Our enquiries continue.

HONG KONG LEE FANS UNITE

The Hong Kong Bruce Lee Club goes from strength to strength. Headed by the redoubtable W. Wong (known to one and all as 'Ah W'), the HKBLC must be one of the most professionally organised Lee associations ever. Leading lights on its committee included Jackson *Bloodsport* Ng, Antony *Dragon* Carpio, Bey *Circus Kid* Logan and the irrepressible Po-Ling Choi. The club has received extensive media coverage in Hong Kong, and is currently planning its opening party, which will be staged at the Hong Kong Convention Centre. Guests will include Donnie Yen, currently shooting a t.v. version of *Fist of Fury*, Bolo Yeung, Carter Wong, Chan Wai Man, Jon Benn, Chaplin Chang, Anders Nelsson and various other local Bruce Lee cognoscenti. As ever, the club invites contacts from overseas Lee fan organisations and from individuals wanting to join. Please address all enquiries, enclosing a reply coupon, to Bey Logan, P.O. Box 83053, San Po Kong Post Office, San Po Kong, Kowloon, Hong Kong.

Lee poses with Nora Miao for a Fist Of Fury publicity shot. His slicked back hair look was later abandoned.

IMPACT 35

IMPACT ACTION MOVIE MAGAZINE

Impact Action Movie Magazine which released its first issue in January 1992, was the final magazine to feature a monthly Bruce Lee Column, and once again this was down to the Editor of Impact, Bey Logan, who had previously been the Editor of Combat Magazine and had written many of the Bruce Lee Columns for them. The first Bruce Lee Column to appear in Impact magazine was dated June 1995 and was written by Bey Logan. The contents of the first column included an article on lost 8mm Bruce Lee footage, with three people stating they had taken the footage of Bruce Lee themselves. One of these rare finds was later released, which was the Ahna Capri Enter the Dragon footage that she took herself on the set. It also had a write-up relating to the newly formed Bruce Lee Hong Kong Fan Club.

With issue 69 of Impact, dated August 1997, the monthly China Beat Column, which focused on Asian movies, had now been turned into a supplement of the same name, and most of the Bruce Lee Columns that appeared during this period would be housed within the supplement. China Beat would run from August 1997 (issue 69) to April 2001 (Issue 112). In the April 2001 issue of Impact, the monthly running of the Bruce Lee Column had been handed over to Andrew Staton, who by now was no longer writing A Finger Pointing and The Bruce and Brandon Lee in the Media Columns for Martial Arts Illustrated. This issue would be the first and last time we got a Bruce Lee in the Media Column within the pages of Impact. By the following month, May 2001 (Issue 113), the Impact team decided to give the magazine a new look, so instead of Impact having the monthly China Beat supplement, the new format magazine would now be equally split into

The Bruce Lee Column

Bey Logan presents a monthly round-up of fresh information on The Little Dragon.

As expected, the Hong Kong Bruce Lee Club is going from strength to strength. After staging an opening party that received saturation media coverage, the club has gone on to organise an exhibition of Bruce Lee memorabilia from around the world. This is being held at the prestigious Hong Kong Arts Centre, and will give local fans a chance to witness the universal popularity of their hero. The exhibition lasts for a whole week, and during that time the club will invite special surprise guests and stage additional events at the Arts Centre, including the first public screening of footage from Donnie Yen's Fist Of Fury remake. Both the 1995 Chen Jun (Donnie) and Petrov (Bey Logan) will be on hand to re-enact their final reel duel. We'll run a full report on the event in next month's column. Meanwhile, in the first of a series of Bruce Lee Remembered articles, kung fu hero Carter Wong shares his reminiscences of The Little Dragon.

For further information on the Hong Kong Bruce Lee Club, please send an s.a.e to: P.O Box 83053, San Po Kong Post Office, San Po Kong, Kowloon, Hong Kong. Please do NOT write anything other than the PO box number, as this will confuse the local postman! Please enclose your name and address, general background and a list of any rare Bruce Lee materials and footage you may have.

BRUCE LEE REMEMBERED (PART ONE)
by Carter Wong

A young Carter Wong poses with Bruce Lee at the 1972 Golden Harvest party.

I first met Bruce Lee when I was just a kid, about twelve years old, because I was friends with his brother, Robert. At that time, the Lee family lived in Nathan Road and I always used to go to that building because a good friend of mine lived next door to them. I was already training in martial arts at the time. I started at the age of eight. Bruce Lee was learning Wing Chun, but he was interested in all different martial arts. I looked on him as an elder brother figure at that time. Later, I met him at 1972 at Golden Harvest studios. I had signed a three-year contract with that company. Samo Hung introduced me to the movie circle. I went to the studio to shoot a screen-test, and Bruce came to see the new martial arts actors. He had a lot of influence at the time. He'd say: "This one is good. This one no good." He remembered me from before. When we were shooting my first film, Hapkido, Bruce came to the set with Chuck Norris and Bob Wall, and we sat down to talk. Bruce gave me a lot of tips on how to kick, how to fight for the camera. They were shooting Way Of The Dragon on the soundstage next door to ours, so sometimes I'd go to watch them film. I hear people wonder why Bruce Lee never got into the ring and fought. I tell you, anyone who saw him rehearse his match with Chuck Norris would have no doubt that he would have been a champion! That wasn't his career, though. He was a movie star. Every year, Golden Harvest used to throw a big party for all their stars. At the end of 1972, we were both at this party, and I had my photograph taken with him. If I'd known he would die so soon, I'd have had more photos taken! I went to visit his house in Kowloon Tong several times. I saw his son, Brandon, at that time. He was just a kid. Bruce liked to have martial artists and stuntmen come to visit. He also used to have a little office at Golden Harvest. He had a one hundred pound weight training bar in there, and he showed me how he could lift it with one hand. In 1973, Bruce went back to visit the States, and when he came back I met him with, Betty Ting Pei and Jhoon Rhee at the Hyatt hotel. Jhoon was in Hong Kong to shoot When Taekwondo Strikes. At that time, Bruce told me he had had his body checked out at UCLA medical centre, and that they told him he had the body of a nineteen-year-old. Very strong! Then he took me up to Jhoon Rhee's suite in the Hyatt and he showed me some kicking and we talked for about an hour and a half. He talked about using me in his last film, Game Of Death. He told me that my part would be one of the heroes, fighting alongside him from the first floor up the pagoda. At that time, he was shooting the fight with Kareem Abdul-Jabbar. Several weeks later, I heard that Bruce Lee died suddenly. I was at home when someone called me. I said: "Come on! you're joking!". I was still with Golden Harvest at the time, and I went to his funeral with the other studio people. Afterwards, the Hong Kong press printed many stories. A great star like him, of course, people will spread rumours. I look on Bruce Lee as the greatest martial arts hero of all time. His success paved the way for people like myself to work in the industry. He also improved the conditions for actors here, which we should all be grateful for. I never tried to copy Bruce Lee. I'd say that my style today has a little of Bruce's shadow cast across it, especially concerning his philosophy and his dedication to hard physical training.

(Carter Wong starred in a huge number of classic kung fu films, including Hapkido, The Skyhawk and When Taekwondo Strikes. In more recent years, he played a major role in the John Carpenter-directed Big Trouble In Little China and in the B movie Hardcase And Fist. He currently resides in Hong Kong.)

The Bruce Lee Column

Bey Logan presents a monthly round-up of fresh information on The Little Dragon.

The current boom in interest in the late Little Dragon continues unabated. As we speak, the epic t.v. remake of Fist Of Fury *is hitting the screens in Hong Kong, with kung fu star Donnie Yen paying his respects to his idol with his portrayal of Chen Jun. The latest word from the U.S. is that tireless Bruce Lee advocate John Little is to release all the 'backyard' training footage in a professional format, under the title* Bruce Lee's Jeet Kune Do. *My own book,* Hong Kong Action Cinema *also features a major overview of The Little Dragon's career, and is out soon from Titan Books. As you can see from the items featured in this month's column, Lee seems to be neither gone nor forgotten. As I write this, I'm within a few miles of Bruce's old Kowloon Tong home and Golden Harvest studios, and it's like he never left town.*

For further information on the Hong Kong Bruce Lee Club(H.K.), please write to it c/o 10/F, Garment Centre, 576-586 Castle Peak Road, Kowloon, Hong Kong (Easyfinder Limited).

THE DRAGON MEETS THE SWEDE

Anders Nelson remembers his brief encounter with Bruce Lee

I first met Bruce through his brother Robert. I was walking in the street and ran into Robert, who I already knew because we were both working in the Hong Kong music industry. He said: "Do you want to go for lunch? I'm having yam cha with my family." I went along, and Bruce was there, along with their other brother, Peter. Bruce turned to me and said: "Are you doing anything this afternoon? We're short of a gweilo (foreigner) on the set (of *Way Of The Dragon*), so why don't you come along and be a baddie?" We went off to the Hammerhill Studios (of Golden Harvest) and there were a number of other westerners already there working. The only person I can remember is a New Zealander, a maori, Mark Mettakingi, whom I also knew from the music side of things. I had a great time. I had known who Bruce Lee was, of course, but I wasn't into that genre. I hadn't actually seen any of his films. I kept protesting that I had no acting or fighting ability, but Bruce just said "Just do what we tell you to do". That turned out to be to hold a stick, go for Bruce with it in this alleyway and then get knocked to the ground with his nunchaku. I actually got grazed by the nunchaku, so that it split my lip, and went to the doctor, and, by coincidence, that was the same doctor who was called on to treat Bruce when he was dying, a year or so later. When you're in shock, you don't feel pain, and actually it hurt much more when Bruce kept grabbing my hand and going "I'm sorry, man! I'm sorry!", he was squeezing my hand so hard. That hurt more than the nunchaku did! The other westerners were generally travellers, people who were just passing through

town. As I remember, I only ever worked that one day. I remember that Bruce never stopped. We'd have breaks for lighting changes and so on, and he'd never take a moment's rest. I remember one time he put a Coke can up on the rafters, a good fifteen feet off the floor, and he spent the whole break trying to kick it. He wouldn't give up 'til he got it, then he'd put it a few inches higher and try again. That was something that really impressed me, that non-stop effort. I never saw Bruce again, but I did go and see *Way Of The Dragon*, just to see myself. I had such a small part in the film. Cough and you miss me! I never thought I'd have people come up to me and say: "Can I touch the hand that touched Bruce Lee?", but that has happened!

(Anders Nelson has lived in Hong Kong all of his life. He was involved in the local music industry since his schooldays, and currently operates a multi-faceted music company called The Media Bank. He believes his greatest accomplishment was not appearing in a Bruce Lee film, but rather bringing the music of Elvis to China!)

Price UK 15p. cartoonic series

two halves, with one half being the normal Impact Magazine and when you flipped the magazine over, you now had the new improved China Beat, now called, Impact East. Mike Leeder, who had taken over the Editorial of the magazine from Bey Logan in issue 101, dated April 2000, was still the Editor of Impact East, and as part of the new overhaul, the new improved Bruce Lee Column had now been turned into a multipage supplement within Impact East called Dragon Power, written by Andrew Staton. Some of the early articles included the following:

The Bruce Lee Column

Column 1- The Super 8 Archive of Lost Footage: and Hong Kong Lee Fan's Unite.
Column 2 - The Orphan Adopted, information on the early Bruce Lee film that had been recently found in colour. Also, there is a write-up on the opening of the Bruce Lee Hong Kong Club.

Column 3 - Bruce Lee Hong Kong Club hold Foundation Ceremony, information on the opening with Po-Ling Choi.
Column 4 - Bruce Lee Remembered Part One, with Carter Wong sharing his memories of Bruce.
Column 5 - Bruce Lee Remembered Part Two, with Anders Nelson sharing his memories of Bruce.
Column 6 - Robin Remembers, Burt Ward talking about his infamous onscreen duel with Bruce in the Batman TV series. The Empty Cup Filled, a small review of the Bruce Lee documentary Jeet Kune Do.
Column 7 - Bruce Lee Betrayed, talking about Bruce Lee's friend Unicorn Chan betraying him on the set of Fist of the Unicorn.
Column 8 - Impact Magazines Bruce Lee Scoop, which detailed Jackie Chan being spotted early on in Fist of Fury, in scenes fans had overlooked.
Column 9 - Norris Shares Bruce Lee Commemorative Stamp, featuring Bruce and Chuck on a First Day Cover released in the UK. On the Dragons Secret Service, what looks like a replica of Bruce's Game of Death tracksuit is spotted in George Lazenby's Bond movie, On Her Majesty's Secret Service.
Column 10 - Highs and Lows, detailing the death of director Lo Wei at the age of 76.

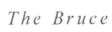

The Bruce Lee Column

RE-ENTER
LEE'S CLASSIC IN CANTONESE

Bey Logan presents a monthly round-up of fresh information on The Little Dragon.

The Hong Kong Bruce Lee Club just staged a brace of events: an artwork awards ceremony (in which members were given prizes for their drawings and paintings of The Little Dragon), which was accompanied by a screening of a pristine print of that ultra-rare early docu, Bruce Lee; The Life, The Legend. Watch out for a full review of this lost artefact in next month's column. The club then held a display of Lee memorabilia, including the artwork executed by its talented membership. It's great to see Lee is still remembered in his home territory. This year's Oscar ceremony was enlivened by the surprise double act of Jackie Chan and Kareem Abdul-Jabbar, and by a clip from Game Of Death. Hard to believe though this may be, most of the Academy members were unaware that the basketball great had acted in a martial arts flick! It was nice to see Bruce appear at such a prestigious event. Had he lived, there's every chance that it would have been HIM up there with Jabbar! Incidentally, the Lee/Jabbar fight also turns up in Jackie Chan's City Hunter as watching the duel 'teaches' Chan how to defeat two towering black opponents.

For further information on the Hong Kong Bruce Lee Club (H.K.), please write c/o 10/F, Garment Centre, 576-586 Castle Peak Road, Kowloon, Hong Kong (Easyfinder Limited).

In dubbing the English language *Enter* into Chinese, the *Golden Harvest* dubbers changed a few minor details with regard to the dialogue, taking certain lines and dropping in some where none had existed before. For example, in the banquet scene, the dialogue between Roper and his female companions, absent from the American print, is very clear. Conversely, in a later scene, after Lee has killed Ohara, Williams jogs up some stone steps past Roper, and says "Hey, Roper, I'll see you in half an hour". In the Chinese print, they pass silently. The very beginning of Roper's introductory fight with Pat

Johnson and the other hoods is cut slightly different in the Chinese print. Roper mouths a line that is not dubbed. The sinister chords that Lalo Schifrin composed for the opening of that scene are also missing, and the music's absence makes you realise how effective it was. The opening and closing credits are completely different. In the international print, the credits run over footage of a 'plane landing at Kai Tak, Williams disembarking, Williams and Roper making their way back through Hong Kong's busy streets. On the Chinese print, we get black-and white shots of Lee, animated in the Monty Python style, intercut with colour stills from *Enter*. The final black-and-white shot is, oddly enough, a still from *Fist of Fury*. On this print, Lee shares his 'Martial Arts Instructor' (i.e.Choreographer) credit with *Mr.Vampire* star Lam Cheng Ying, here billed in the Mandarin version of his name : 'Lin Cheng Ying'.Where the closing credits on the American print run over footage of Han's tiger claw hand embedded in his throne, the Chinese print freeze-

frames when Lee notices the claws, then a shaky credit roll appears, in which Bob Wall's character is billed, erroneously, as 'Okata'. After Lee died, *Golden Harvest* decided to postpone the release of the Mandarin print of *Enter the Dragon*, rushing into production with the very first Bruce Lee docmentary, *Bruce Lee ; The Life, The Legend*. The docu featured extensive footage from Lee's funeral (as Raymond Chow had assigned a camera crew to follow the proceedings from Hong Kong all the way to Seattle) and lengthy clips from *Enter*, which, at that time, no one in Hong Kong had ever seen.

Given the Bruce Lee fever then gripping the territory, the documentary performed very well. *Enter the Dragon*, however, posted disappointing box office results. Though by no means a flop, it failed to match the takings of *Way of the Dragon*, the most successful of the Lee films in Hong Kong. *Enter the Dragon* is the only one of the completed Bruce Lee's movies that plays better in English than Chinese, for obvious reasons. If your Chinese print of *Enter* is in the Mandarin dialect, then that's a copy of the 'original' version. The Cantonese edition, originally distributed in Asia via *Golden Harvest*'s deal with the Virgin Vision, is a later release. In whatever language, though, *Enter* remains unique, in that it manages to combine superlative martial artistry with decent production values and a cohesive plot, something no other East/West co production has managed. It captured the magic of Bruce Lee at the height of his powers, and, twenty-three years on, that magic still glows like fine jade in an ageing casket.

IMPACT 23

By the early millennium, magazine sales were falling, due to the birth of the internet, and with new information on Bruce Lee becoming sparser; the Bruce Lee Column began to fade out of existence. It has now been around twenty years since the last regular Bruce Lee Column appeared, and so with the rebirth of Eastern Heroes Magazine, it was decided by the team to start a new Bruce Lee Column, dedicated to the most famous Martial Arts Movie Star in the World, the legendary, Bruce Lee.

The Bruce Lee Column

Bey Logan presents a monthly round-up of fresh information on The Little Dragon.

ROBIN REMEMBERS
Burt Ward on a *Life In Tights* and a duel with The Dragon

The Bruce Lee Column

Bey Logan presents a monthly round-up of fresh information on The Little Dragon.

The Hong Kong Bruce Lee Fan Club celebrated its one year anniversary with a party at the local Planet Hollywood. The eaterie features a number of Little Dragon artefacts, and we'll be running a photo feature on them in an upcoming column. Suspended from the ceiling is one of the Black Beauty cars used in the Green Hornet t.v. series, but, to the relief of all, Bey Logan and Antony Carpio have agreed NOT to reprise their Britt Reid and Kato roles, played so memorably at the recent Lee memorabilia exhibition in Wanchai. Bruce is definitely back in Hong Kong with a vengeance. He is one of four Chinese stars featured on a postage stamp release. This philatelic celebration of the Dragon hit H.K. post offices on November 15th, which is my birthday and MY initials are also 'B.L.'. A coincidence? Perhaps not. (Cue X Files theme). Speaking of myself, as usual!, my book Hong Kong Action Cinema is in a store near you now, and features an extensive section of The Little Dragon. I'm now back at work on my next magnum opus, a Lee Siu Lung volume entitled Bruce Lee: The Hong Kong Years. *Meanwhile, following the success of Jet Lee's* Fist Of Legend *and Donnie Yen's t.v.* Fist Of Fury, *two new movie versions of Cheng Mo Man are set to go before the cameras. The first is a new* Fist Of Fury 2 *starring the aforementioned Yenster, and the second a* Fist *spin-off featuring 70's kung fu hero Leung Siu Lung.*

For further information on the Hong Kong Bruce Lee Club(H.K.), please write to it c/o 10/F, Garment Centre, 576-586 Castle Peak Road, Kowloon, Hong Kong (Easyfinder Limited).

IMPACT BRUCE LEE SCOOP!

Jackie Chan sighted in *Fist Of Fury*!

Of course the young Jackie is in *Fist*. Many articles, interviews and documentaries have already made mention of the fact that Chan doubled for the Japanese sensei, Suzuki, who gets kicked through a shoji screen by Chen Jun (Bruce Lee) at the end of the movie. However, even viewers with the most sophisticated freeze frame available would be hard-pressed to identify this flying stuntman as Chan. However, Jackie Chan stuntman and long-time Bruce Lee buff Antony Carpio points out that Jackie is very much in evidence earlier in the picture. Just after Bruce Lee's famous destruction of the 'No Dogs or Chinese' sign, the action cuts to the Chung Wu school, where his classmates are undergoing their 'lin gung' or daily workout regime. In the first shot, Chan is at left of frame, in a mixed bow stance, wearing a grey kung fu suit with white undershirt. He's sparring with a girl who wears a dark blue outfit. He punches at her, and she kicks at him. They move around in a clockwise direction. We cut away to the other trainees, then Jackie is visible again, just after we pan past Nora Miao practising a solo form.

Jackie who? Bruce Lee provided an early payday for the young Chan.

The girl, who seems to be using mainly Crane boxing techniques, jump kicks at Chan, and they exchange blows, still moving in a clockwise direction. We cut to Tien Feng, as he watches the activity approvingly. Then when we see the Japanese fighters arrive to 'tek kwoon', to attack the school, Chan vanishes from the scene. He appears again (briefly) during the melee that follows, doubling for James Tien when Tien's character executes a breakdance style series of foot sweeps.

Fist Of Fury *gave an early starring role to Nora Miao, who appeared opposite Jackie Chan in Lo Wei's 'official' sequel.*

Don't concentrate on the finger!: Bruce Lee in Fist.

So why has this early Chan sighting gone unrecognised for so long? One of the main reasons is that Jackie is virtually unrecognisable. *Fist* was shot long before he had an eye-widening operation and had his teeth capped. He's also skinnier here than in his later films. Another reason is that most viewers, like me, tend to fast-forward through the non-Bruce Lee scenes of his films! Finally, there's the fact that Chan himself, perhaps embarrassed at having once been a 'keh leh fai', an extra, has never admitted that he appeared in this scene.

The Bruce Lee Column

Bey Logan presents a monthly round-up of fresh information on The Little Dragon.

Much fun was had at the recent Planet Hollywood bash hosted by the Hong Kong Bruce Lee Club. The event saw over 240 local Little Dragonheads gather to celebrate the life and work of their hero. As ever, our own Bey The Beast was the sole westerner visible! Guests of honour included Donnie t.v. Fist of Fury *Yen, RTHK broadcaster Lot Sze and a number of other local names. The fun and games included a Bruce Lee video quiz and the arrival of a giant Little Dragon birthday cake. The masters of ceremonies were stuntmen Antony* Thunderbolt *Carpio and Jackson* Bloodsport *Ng. Given that such events are relatively commonplace elsewhere in the world, it's nice to see Bruce Lee given some recognition in his native territory. Elsewhere in Hong Kong, the Bruce Lee-related features proceed apace, with both Donnie Yen and 80s kung fu movie and t.v. actor Leung Siu Lung preparing big-screen* Fist of Fury *sequels. Surprise casting in the Yen version is the presence of MediaAsia honcho Nicholas James as the snivelling interpreter played by Wei Ping-ou in the original Golden Harvest film. MediaAsia, coincidentally, handles the rights to all the Golden Harvest Bruce Lee films, including* Fist of Fury. *James, formally a producer at TVB, is fluent in Mandarin. Will Bey Logan reprise his t.v.* Fist *role, that of the Russian fighter played by Bob Baker in the original? "Only if I get to beat up Nicholas James!", he quips.*

For further information on the Hong Kong Bruce Lee Club(H.K.), please write to it c/o 10/F, Garment Centre, 576-586 Castle Peak Road, Kowloon, Hong Kong (Easyfinder Limited).

NORRIS SHARES LEE COMMEMORATIVE STAMP

Walker: Texas Ranger star Chuck Norris, who began his acting career as a bad guy in Bruce's *Way of the Dragon*, gets to share The Little Dragon's Hong Kong postage stamp, which was released on November 15th, 1995. The shot used depicts Lee and Norris posing for a promotional still during the filming of their epic Coliseum duel. This may mark the first time in British history that a living person other than the reigning monarch was featured on a stamp! The first day cover sold out within hours, with long queues at all post offices. The release actually included three other stamps with three other deceased Chinese performers honoured. However, most of the media attention was focused on Bruce.

Chuck Norris joins Lee on the Little Dragon's stamp.

A bearded Lee: he never got to work with the equally hirsute George Lazenby.

ON THE DRAGON'S SECRET SERVICE

This may be supposition, but, on a recent re-viewing of George Lazenby's sole outing as James Bond (see article elsewhere this issue), we couldn't help notice that Lazenby, and several other characters, wear form-fitting ski suits similar in style to the one-piece tracksuit sported by Bruce Lee in *Game of Death*. The aforementioned item is yellow with a black stripe down the side, as are the jackets worn by Blofeld's henchmen in *OHMSS*. Coincidence? We know Lee saw the 1969 007 flick, prior to starting work on *G.O.D.*. Incidentally, the luckless Lazenby appeared on Robert Chua's long-running variety show *Enjoy Yourself Tonight* the evening before The Little Dragon's untimely demise, and announced that he had just signed the deal to make a film with Bruce Lee. The same journalist who booked George onto *EYT* also had the unhappy task of calling to tell him that Lee had died.

Bruce keeping his hands to himself during an EYT *taping.*

The Bruce Lee Column

Bey Logan presents a monthly round-up of fresh information on The Little Dragon.

Just as I was compiling this month's Bruce Lee special, I read in the Chinese paper Oriental Daily News that director Lo Wei had died. Though he had a stormy relationship with Lee, Lo's contribution to the legend of the Little Dragon cannot be underestimated. In a specially extended Bruce Lee column, we look back at the man and his career.

The Hong Kong Bruce Lee Club rumbles ever forward. Upcoming from the colony's only Little Dragon society are an art contest, with fans displaying their renditions of Bruce, and a film show, which will feature some Lee rarities not seen since the 70's. Unfortunately, only a few overseas fans will be able to attend, but we'll run a full report in these pages. Maybe in the future we can stage a combined event in the U.S. or U.K.

For further information on the Hong Kong Bruce Lee Club(H.K.), please write to it c/o 10/F, Garment Centre, 576-586 Castle Peak Road, Kowloon, Hong Kong (Easyfinder Limited).

HIGHS AND LOWS

The career of the man who directed ***The Big Boss*** and ***Fist Of Fury***.

The death of film director Lo Wei signals the end of an era for Hong Kong cinema. Arguably more prolific than talented and more infamous then revered, this grand old man of the Chinese movie industry died of a heart attack at the age of 76. He was a key figure in the early years of film-making giant Golden Harvest, the director of two of Bruce Lee's four completed films and the man who could justifiably claim to have discovered Jackie Chan.

A native of Shanghai, Lo began his show business career during the Sino-Japanese war. Under the stage name 'Lo Ching', he established himself as a matinee idol and went on to star in a number of early Hong Kong movie productions.

He made a successful shift to a directing career, working at the mighty Shaw Brothers Studio. His films there included *The Shadow Whip*, starring the aforementioned Cheng Pei Pei. Tired of labouring in the shadow of the quintessential Shaws' director, Chang Cheh, Lo accepted

Bruce Lee with the late Lo Wei, the man who brought both Lee and Jackie Chan to the big screen.

Despite this, Lo does not seem to have been regarded with much genuine affection. After his death, stars like Jackie, Cheng Pei and Frank Chan turned out to shed crocodile tears, but it should be noted that few of his former colleagues helped Lo Wei out during the final period of his life, in which bankruptcy brought pressure that undoubtedly contributed to his untimely demise.

His violent falling out with Bruce Lee is better remembered than his contribution to *Big Boss* and *Fist Of Fury*. His films with Jackie Chan all had one thing in common. They flopped. He bears the distinction of being one of the few film-makers to shoot a film so bad (*Slaughter in San Francisco*) that one of its stars (Chuck Norris) sued in an attempt to prevent its re-release.

In brief, Lo was a man capable of snatching defeat from the jaws of victory.

Raymond Chow's offer that he leave the company to join the then-fledgling Golden Harvest.

His early Harvest films included the swordplay actioner *The Invincible Eight*, with soon-to-be Bruce Lee cohorts Nora Miao, James Tien and Angela Mao, *The Comet Strikes* and *The Hurricane* both starring Nora Miao. Legend has it that Lo's son, David, first caught sight of Bruce Lee on the Hong Kong t.v. show *Enjoy Yourself Tonight*. *The Green Hornet* had already played in the territory, and Lee, on a return visit to his hometown, had been invited to show off his kung fu skills.

Lo's then-wife, former actress Liu Liang Hwa, was dispatched to L.A. to sign Bruce to a deal, on behalf of Golden Harvest. Part of the understanding with the company was that Lo Wei would direct Lee. This is why the original

The Bruce Lee Column

Bey Logan presents a monthly round-up of fresh information on The Little Dragon.

It seems that no stone will be left unturned in the current crusade to make even the most obscure Little Dragon material available to his frantic fans. In the U.K., Young Bruce Lee *has already hit the video shelves, offering fans a chance to see rare clips from Lee Siu Lung's earliest movie vehicles. In the U.S., John Little is preparing his Jeet Kune Do book series, and a second Bruce Lee's JKD videotape. In Hong Kong, the Bruce Lee Club is preparing its second major event, at which it is planned to screen the little-seen documentary* Bruce Lee: The Man, The Myth. *This was rushed into production by Golden Harvest shortly after Lee's untimely demise and played, in H.K., on a double-bill with* Enter the Dragon. *It was never released on video in the Far East, though it remains part of the Golden Harvest back catalogue. Word is that a new asian distributor has acquired the rights to all the Bruce Lee footage, including, perhaps, the as-yet-unseen acres of* Game of Death *out-takes. The flood of Dragon pearls continues unabated!*

For further information on the Hong Kong Bruce Lee Club(H.K.), please write to it c/o 10/F, Garment Centre, 576-586 Castle Peak Road, Kowloon, Hong Kong (Easyfinder Limited).

BRUCE LEE BETRAYED

Inside *The Unicorn Fist*

The relationship between Bruce Lee and the late Unicorn Chan was long and deep. Whatever Chan's limitations as an actor and martial artist may have been, The Little Dragon stood by his childhood friend with commendable loyalty. "Where there is Bruce there will be Unicorn", he said, and lived up those words, casting Chan Siu Kay Lin in *Fist of Fury* and *Way of the Dragon*. Their bond was forged when both worked as child actors in the Hong Kong film industry. The recently released compilation *The Young Bruce Lee* features both the beginning and end of their friendship, depicting Unicorn and Bruce in a black-and-white drama and at the press conference to launch *The Unicorn Pal*, Chan's one failed shot at fame as an action hero. The latter project came about when director Tang Di, of the Sing Hoi Film Company, ran into Unicorn in Hong Kong's famed Peninsula Hotel. He put it to Chan that, if he could convince Bruce to choreograph the fights and make a cameo appearance, Unicorn could star in his own feature. Lee took this opportunity to help his old friend, despite the fact that he was busy preparing *Game of Death*. Lee's involvement was more show than substance. He actually directed only a few minutes of action for *The Unicorn Fist*, and provided more support by providing a photo opportunity during a set visit and by helping cast the film with some impressive 'heavies'. These included *Game* players Chi Hon Tsoi and Chieh Yuan, and Bruce's good friend Chan Wai Man, a kung fu champion turned actor. The film itself remains an oddity. As a martial artist of the Wang Yu arm-flailer school, his real physical skill was a gymnast, and he shows off his flipping ability to good effect. The cast featured several players who would go on to better things. Jackie Chan, who performed stunts on the picture, has a walk-on role as one of a gang of punks who tease Unicorn. Also on hand were actor/stuntman Mars, later Jackie's right-hand man, and Mung Hoi, who starred in a number of films in his own right (most memorably *The Buddha Assassinator*) and almost became Mr Cynthia Rothrock! Yasuaki Kurata, who played a Japanese fighter, is still very active, with a great role in last year's *Fist of Legend*, opposite Jet Lee. Other Bruce Lee movie veterans include *Fist* interpreter Wei Ping Ou and a muscular westerner who played one of the men who shoot Chen Jun (Bruce Lee) at the end of that picture. When the finished film was released, Lee was horrified that footage of him had been shot on the set, without his knowledge, and spliced into *The Unicorn Fist*. The posters for the movie also gave an unrealistic impression of Bruce's involvement in the project. The incident caused a major rift between the life-long friends, and may explain why Unicorn was noticeably absent from *Enter the Dragon*. Regardless of Lee's objections, the film was released worldwide, and can be found under a variety of titles, including *The Unicorn Pal*, *Bruce Lee and I*, *Fist of Unicorn* and *Force of Bruce Lee's Fist*.

Bruce flexes on the Unicorn *set alongside the young Mung Hoi.*

Happier times: Bruce at the Unicorn Fist *press conference at H.K's Mirimar Hotel.*

The Official Voice Of the Bruce and Brandon Lee Association

DRAGON POWER

The Crow
Stairway To Heaven Re-released on Video

Unbeatable Footage
Rare Bruce Lee Trailer Archive Released

The Unbeatable Bruce Lee

Showdown In Little Tokyo
Released On DVD

Way Of The Dragon
We Look At The Making Of This Classic

DRAGON POWER

The Official Voice Of the Bruce and Brandon Lee Association

Bruce Lee In
Blondie

Plus: Wende Wagner Interviewed & Brandon Lee Quest Launched

THE OFFICIAL VOICE OF THE BRUCE AND BRANDON LEE ASSOCIATION

DRAGON POWER

Goodbye Bruce Lee

Bruce Li Stars In A Version Of Game Of Death
Surprisingly Close To Bruce Lee's Original Concept

Plus: New Asylum Action Figure Reviewed & Anniversary TV Screenings

Fury Of The
Dragon

DRAGON POWER

Digital Dragon
Bruce Lee On X-Box P...

Bruce Lee
The Immortal Dragon

Bruce Lee:
Quest Of The Dragon
Event...

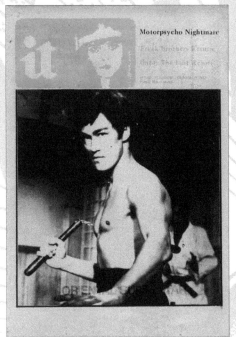

Motorpsycho Nightmare

SEPTEMBER 1980 No 5 60p

Music & Video

VIDEO CAMERA SURVEY
PAGE 60

ASIAN VIDEO:
BIG BUCKS AND DIRTY TRICKS.
NEWEST POPWAVE IS ELECTRONIC.
TELEVISION'S FIVE RING CIRCUS.
ROCK DESPERADOS:
DALTREY AND FAITH IN McVICAR.

AFTER BRUCE LEE, THE CLONE INDUSTRY.

FOLD-OUT POSTERMAGAZINE

Lee exposed **Bruce Lee**
THE KING OF KUNG FU

HOW DID THE LITTLE DRAGON DIE?

Bruce Lee Lord of the Leap EXPOSED by Dan Slater

GIANT POSTER INSIDE approx. 2' x 3'

N° 1/8
Film-Star-Series.
periodical
English Edition.
UK 25p.

october 1973 40p

films and **filming**

BRUCE LEE *Enter the Dragon*

REVIEW JULY 1974 10p

BRUCE LEE POSTERS

KARATE
& Oriental Arts MARCH/APRIL 1974

KUNG FU

No. 47 30p

THE BEST IN MARTIAL ARTS COVERAGE

50p

COMBAT

Vol.1 No.1 September 1974

Britain's Most Exciting NEW Magazine

The Art of Kung-Fu
(Part one)

Valera Talks of
Come Back

A History of
Unarmed Combat

Approx. 2' x 3'

Price UK 15p.

cartoonic

series –

STRIP! INSIDE

PLUS: The facts about Bruce Lee

FIGHTERS' MONTHLY

50p
Vol 1 No 1

THE MAGAZINE FOR THE TRUE MARTIAL ARTS ENTHUSIAST

BRUCE LEE
The Truth

MEIJI SUZUKI - Advanced Katas

PLUS
Shorinji Kempo
AND
The PFKO Championship

VICTOR KAN - Vingtsun Kung Fu

Price UK 15p.
cartoonic
series -

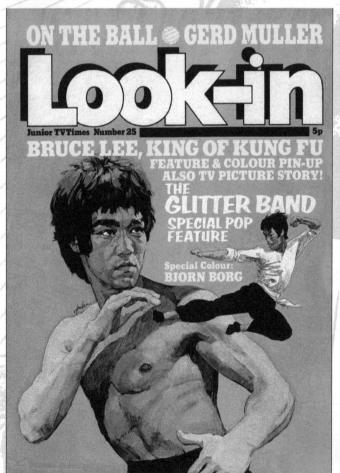

on earth
survive the
fury that was
Bruce Lee!

THE BIG BOSS COLLECTOR

By John Negron
U.S.A. Collector Extrordinaire

Once again my good friend John Negron opens the doors to showcase
some of the items he has collected over the years. This issue we
take a look at the many items that represent Bruce Lee first big
blockbuster movie "the Big Boss" also known in the U.S.A as "Fist
of Fury". That epic flying kick that we see in the final reel of the
movie has become an iconic logo appearing in articles and used like
a trade mark with certain items. I enjoy showcasing these items,
often because I see many items that I did not know existed. It also
allows other collectors the opportunity to see what items still eludes
their own collections, as Bruce lee memorabilia has become a great
investment through the decades especially items from the 70s, and
items before his death fetch premium money especially magazines.
So please enjoy the fruits and passion of Johns collecting and
hopefully we will be showcasing more in the next issue.

VIDEOS
&
LASERDISCS

FISTS OF FURY

ISBN # 1-55510-913-6

Legendary kung fu master Bruce Lee unleashes the awesome power and fury of his full martial arts expertise in this violent, action packed adventure tale about a young Chinese man called upon to defend his family's honor. But, when he sets out to avenge the murder of his cousin, Lee uncovers a terrifying secret that places his own life in jeopardy and sets the stage for a violent and brutal confrontation from which only one can emerge the winner.

CAST
Bruce Lee
Miao Ker Hsiu
Robert Baker
James Tien
Written and Directed by Lo Wei

COLOR

WE MAKE COLLECTIBILITY A WAY OF LIFE

Approx. 100 Minutes

© 1993 GoodTimes Home Video Corp.
16 E. 40 St., New York, NY 10016
All rights reserved.

VHS
8472

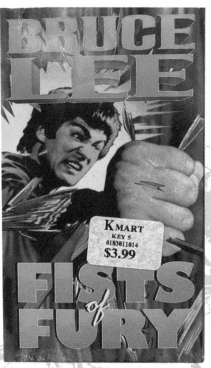

Chang (Bruce Lee) swears on his mother's locket never to fight again and moves to the mainland in search of a new life with his long lost relatives. When he accepts a job in an ice house, he accidentally uncovers that the business is a front for drug smugglers. It's up to Chang and his Kung Fu cousins to confront the unlawful owners and break their ring of power over the city.

When Chang's cousins are ambushed and murdered by the drug lords, he must decide whether to honor his mother's wishes or unleash his bridled Fists of Fury!

STARRING BRUCE LEE MARIA YI JAMES TIEN NORA MIAO
DIRECTOR LO WEI
Running Time: 100 minutes in color

WARNING: CONTAINS NUDITY & GRAPHIC VIOLENCE. MAY NOT BE SUITABLE FOR ALL VIEWERS.

©MCMXCIV GEMSTONE ENTERTAINMENT
DESIGN, GRAPHICS & PACKAGE
ALL RIGHTS RESERVED
MADE IN THE USA GUARANTEED SUPERIOR QUALITY

...ACTION, ACTION, ACTION!!

The master of karate / kung-fu is back!

FISTS OF FURY

Lee quickly discovers that his new job at an icebox factory requires some detective work. Why are relatives and friends who also work in the plant mysteriously disappearing? The trail leads into the jaws of a vicious, and of course, well-armed drug smuggling gang. Lee must pit his formidable martial arts skills against a scheming drug lord and his army of henchmen in order to protect family, friends and himself. The stakes are raised when Lee's love interest is carried off to be the villain's latest conquest. Lee has one difficult bridge to cross, however - he has taken a solemn vow of non-violence! A rapid-fire tale of love, loyalty and good versus evil, Fists of Fury delivers an array of affable good guys, despicable foes and impressive combat scenes.

THE CHINESE CONNECTION

In the exotic, ethnic melting pot of Shanghai, the revered master of a Chinese combat school dies in mysterious circumstances. To add to the students' grief, a local Japanese martial arts school comes forward with taunts and racist insults. Lee portrays a young student who vows to uncover the truth behind his beloved teacher's death. Lee's mission unleashes the fanatical rage of foes bent on utterly destroying his school. Using a variety of weapons as well as his equally lethal hands and feet, Lee engages in mortal combat with a series of colorful and thoroughly unpleasant enemies. From an emotion-laden opening scene to the surprise ending, this movie delivers all the action, romance and intrigue that Lee fans have come to expect.

- FEATURE
- SCENE INDEX
- BIOGRAPHY
- MARTIAL ARTS
- PHILOSOPHY
- TRIVIA

COLLECTOR'S EDITION
Bruce Lee
every limb of his body is a lethal weapon in
"Fists of Fury"

KARATE/ KUNG-FU!

The new screen excitement that gives you the biggest kick of your life!

SHOUT SELECT

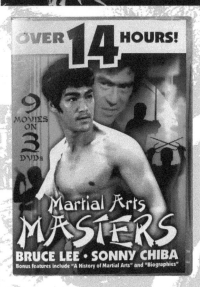

ブルース・リー

BOOKS & MAGAZINES

BRUCE LEE

unstoppable!
unbelievable!
unbeatable!

THE MASTER OF KUNG FU
WILL break you up.
smash you down and kick you apart with

"THE CHINESE CONNECTION"

WATCH FOR IT AT THE STATE — SOON

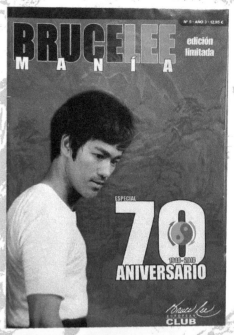

BRUCE LEE MANÍA
edición limitada

ESPECIAL
70 ANIVERSARIO
1940–2010

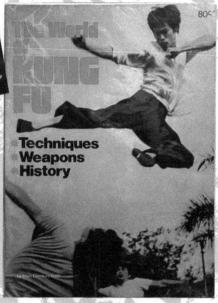

The World of
KUNG FU

* Techniques
* Weapons
* History

BRUCE LEE MANÍA
edición limitada

JPF&T
The Journal of Popular Film and Television
9/1 $3.00

BRUCE LEE MANÍA
edición limitada

BRUCE LEE MANÍA
edición limitada

LA REVISTA DE LAS ARTES MARCIALES

DOJO

Nº 228 - AÑO XXI - 350 Pts.

LAS AMERICAS
PRECIO **6** SOLES

Qué opinan sobre

Bruce Lee

las estrellas del cine
de Artes Marciales

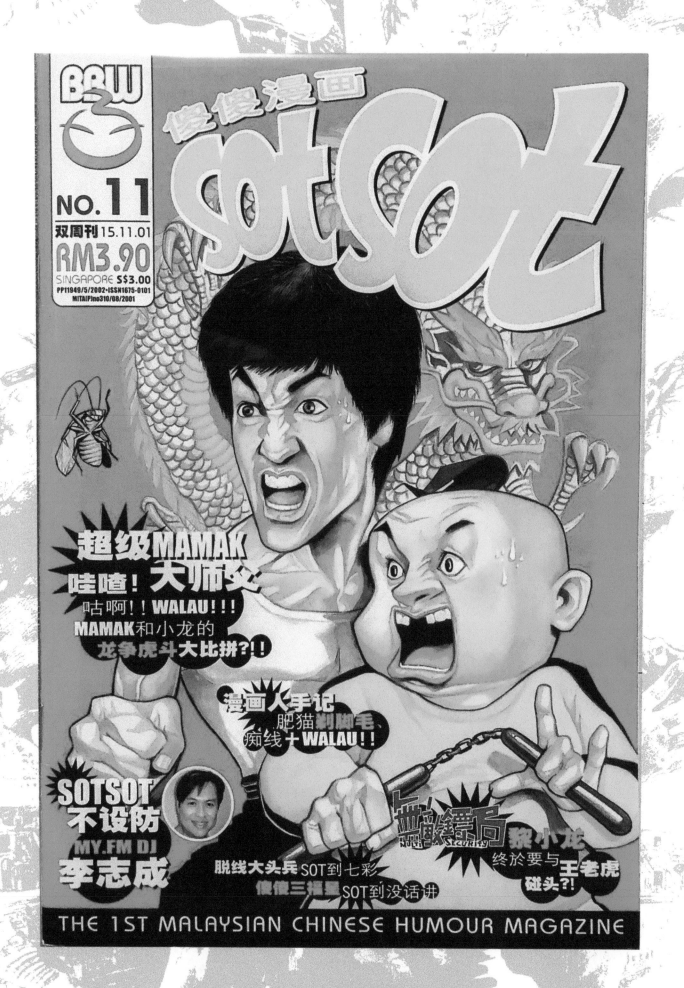

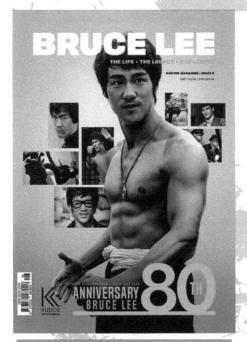

BRUCE LEE
THE LIFE · THE LEGACY · THE LEGEND
POSTER MAGAZINE / ISSUE 8

ANNIVERSARY
BRUCE LEE
80th

THE
WARRIOR
WITHIN

THE PHILOSOPHIES OF BRUCE LEE

BY JOHN LITTLE   Foreword by Linda Lee Cadwell

OFFICIAL COLLECTOR'S EDITION
BRUCE LEE®
VOL. 6

IN HIS OWN WORDS
LETTERS, JOURNALS AND PERSONAL INSIGHT FROM THE BRUCE LEE ARCHIVE

INTRODUCTION BY SHANNON LEE

SECRETS OF
KUNG FU

A TRAVEL TO REMEMBER BRUCE LEE
功夫秘奥

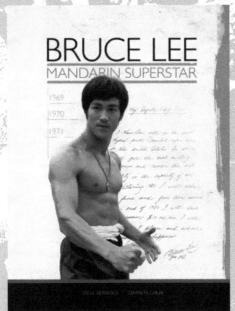

BRUCE LEE
MANDARIN SUPERSTAR

1969
1970
1971

Bruce Lee

Wisdom for the Way

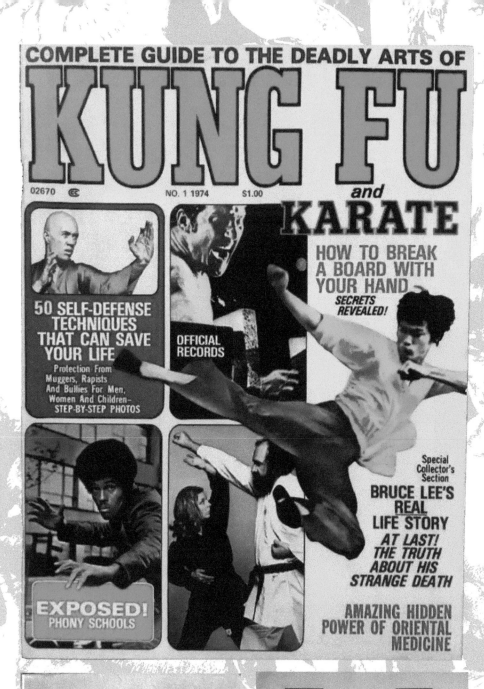

COMPLETE GUIDE TO THE DEADLY ARTS OF

KUNG FU

02670   NO. 1 1974 $1.00

and

KARATE

50 SELF-DEFENSE TECHNIQUES THAT CAN SAVE YOUR LIFE
Protection From Muggers, Rapists And Bullies For Men, Women And Children— STEP-BY-STEP PHOTOS

OFFICIAL RECORDS

HOW TO BREAK A BOARD WITH YOUR HAND
SECRETS REVEALED!

Special Collector's Section
BRUCE LEE'S REAL LIFE STORY
AT LAST! THE TRUTH ABOUT HIS STRANGE DEATH

AMAZING HIDDEN POWER OF ORIENTAL MEDICINE

EXPOSED! PHONY SCHOOLS

DIE SPINNE
KRIMINALROMAN

Nr. 170   DM 1,20

Gefährlicher Zauber

BRUCE LEE

N° 22 $ 1500

POSTER INEDITO DE LEE

Declaraciones EXCLUSIVAS de BRUCE

ΑΙΓΟΚΕΡΩΣ/ΚΙΝΗΜΑΤΟΓΡΑΦΙΚΟ ΑΡΧΕΙΟ 53

Μπρους Λη

INTERNATIONAL
BRUCE LEE
& BRANDON LEE
ASSOCIATION TIMES

BRUCE LEE

THE TREASURES OF
BRUCE LEE
李小龍
THE OFFICIAL STORY OF THE LEGENDARY MARTIAL ARTIST

BY PAUL BOWMAN
FOREWORD BY SHANNON LEE

"KNOWING IS NOT ENOUGH"

The Official Newsletter of
Jun Fan Jeet Kune Do / Bruce Lee Educational Foundation

Spring 1999 • Vol. 3, No. 1 • ISSN: 1033-1325

INSIDE THIS ISSUE . . .

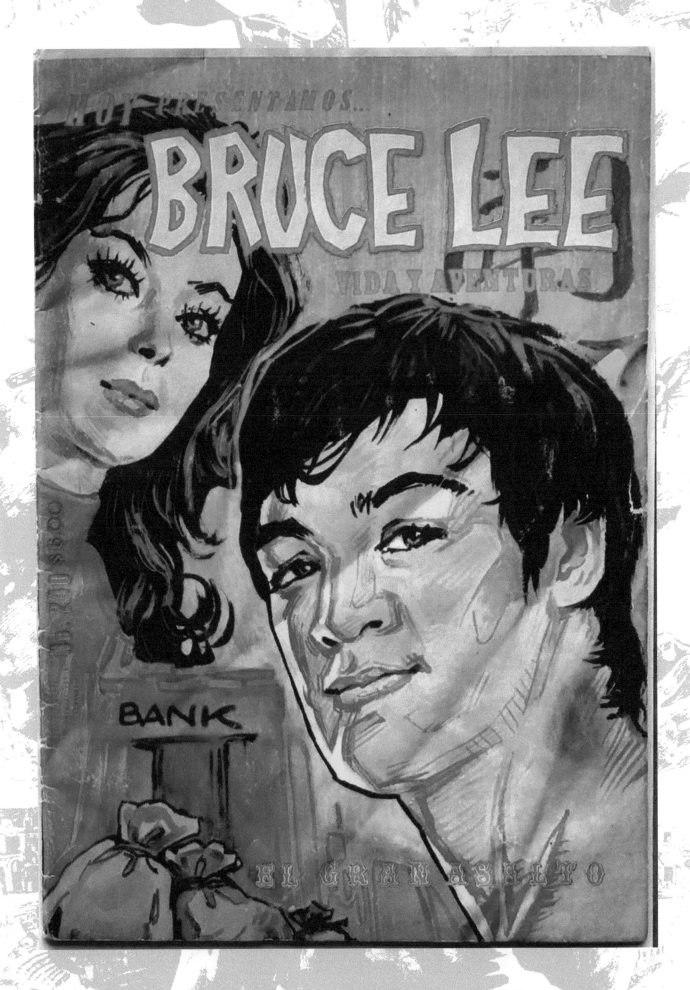

李小龍被謀財害命？

丁珮大爆內幕

$1.50
壹元伍角

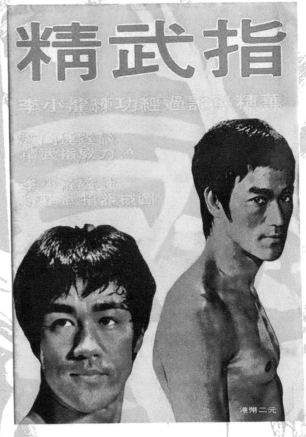

精武指

李小龍練功經過詳盡 精華

港幣二元

CULTURE ET ART, MARTIAUX D'ASIE

DRAGON N°16
MAGAZINE

BRUCE LEE
La Flûte Silencieuse son film inachevé

BUDO
Zen et Karaté

KUNG FU
Rencontre avec M° Yang Jwing Ming

DÉCOUVERTE
Le Shorinji Kempo

MÉDECINE
Shiatsu : la santé au bout des doigts

JAPON
Le festival des samourais à Osaka

EXPOSITION
L'amour au temps des geishas

NEUROCOMBAT
Comment le cerveau réagit en état de stress

M 06506 -16-F: 7,00 € -RD

李小龍 暴斃內幕

＊每册港幣式元正

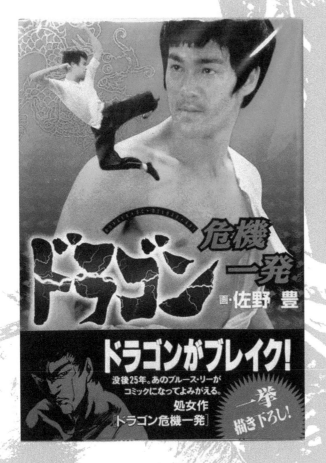

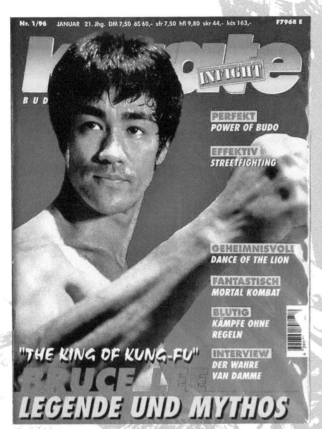

BRUCE LEE
ILIMITADO

MARCOS OCAÑA RIZO

BRUCE LEE
COLLECTOR

N°1

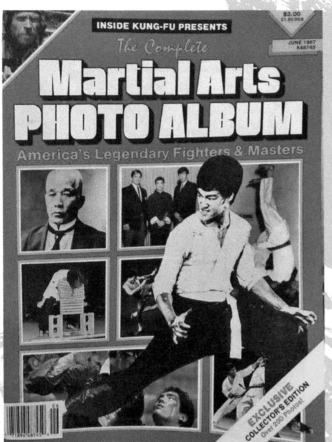

INSIDE KUNG-FU PRESENTS

The Complete

Martial Arts PHOTO ALBUM

America's Legendary Fighters & Masters

$3.00
£1.85 DGS

JUNE 1987
K48745

EXCLUSIVE COLLECTOR'S EDITION
Over 200 Photos!

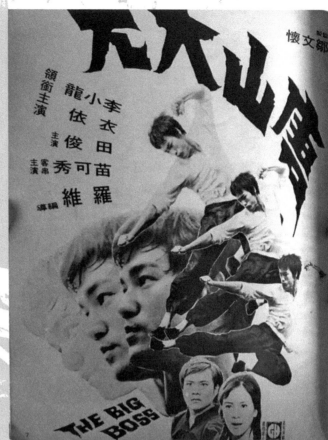

鄒文懷

領銜主演　龍依俊　小衣田苗

主演　秀可維羅

客串主演

編導

THE BIG BOSS

HERITAGE

ENTERTAINMENT & MUSIC
MEMORABILIA AUCTION
JULY 16-18, 2021 | DALLAS

BRUCE LEE:
THE AUCTION

SPECIAL DE !

BRUCE LEE

LA HISTORIA DE SU VIDA Y SU ARTE

EDICION SPECIAL PELICULA COMPLETA

EL GRAN JEFE

LOBBY CARDS

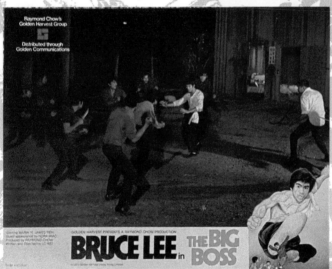

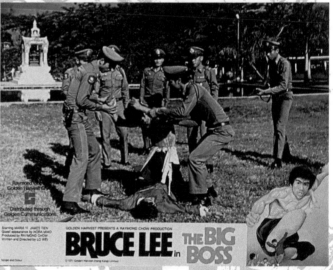

Raymond Chow's Golden Harvest Group

Distributed through Golden Communications

Starring MARIA YI, JAMES TIEN
Guest appearances by NORA MIAO
Produced by RAYMOND CHOW
Written and Directed by LO WEI

GOLDEN HARVEST PRESENTS A RAYMOND CHOW PRODUCTION

BRUCE LEE in **THE BIG BOSS**

©1971 Golden Harvest (Hong Kong) Limited

Raymond Chow's Golden Harvest Group

Distributed through Golden Communications

Starring MARIA YI, JAMES TIEN
Guest appearance by NORA MIAO
Produced by RAYMOND CHOW
Written and Directed by LO WEI

GOLDEN HARVEST PRESENTS A RAYMOND CHOW PRODUCTION

BRUCE LEE in **THE BIG BOSS**

Scope and Colour

©1971 Golden Harvest (Hong Kong) Limited

KARATE KUNG-FU!

The oriental sensation – now gives America the action its been waiting for!

Bruce Lee

every limb of his body is a lethal weapon in

"**Fists of Fury**"

National General Pictures presents Bruce Lee in "FISTS OF FURY" • Produced by Raymond Chow
Screenplay and Direction by Lo Wei • Color • A National General Pictures Release ® R RESTRICTED

73/112

KARATE KUNG-FU!

The oriental sensation – now gives America the action its been waiting for!

Bruce Lee

every limb of his body is a lethal weapon in

"**Fists of Fury**"

National General Pictures presents Bruce Lee in "FISTS OF FURY" • Produced by Raymond Chow
Screenplay and Direction by Lo Wei • Color • A National General Pictures Release ® R RESTRICTED

73/112

KARATE KUNG-FU!

The oriental sensation— now gives America the action its been waiting for!

Bruce Lee

every limb of his body is a lethal weapon in

"Fists of Fury"

National General Pictures presents Bruce Lee in "FISTS OF FURY" • Produced by Raymond Chow
Screenplay and Direction by Lo Wei • Color • A National General Pictures Release

73/112

KARATE KUNG-FU!

The oriental sensation— now gives America the action its been waiting for!

Bruce Lee

every limb of his body is a lethal weapon in

"Fists of Fury"

National General Pictures presents Bruce Lee in "FISTS OF FURY" • Produced by Raymond Chow
Screenplay and Direction by Lo Wei • Color • A National General Pictures Release

73/112

KARATE
KUNG-FU!

The oriental
sensation —
now gives
America the
action its
been
waiting for!

Bruce
Lee

every limb of his body
is a lethal weapon in

"Fists of Fury"

National General Pictures presents Bruce Lee in "FISTS OF FURY" • Produced by Raymond Chow
Screenplay and Direction by Lo Wei • Color • A National General Pictures Release ⑧ Ⓡ RESTRICTED

73/112

KARATE
KUNG-FU!

The oriental
sensation —
now gives
America the
action its
been
waiting for!

Bruce
Lee

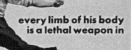

every limb of his body
is a lethal weapon in

"Fists of Fury"

National General Pictures presents Bruce Lee in "FISTS OF FURY" • Produced by Raymond Chow
Screenplay and Direction by Lo Wei • Color • A National General Pictures Release ⑧ Ⓡ RESTRICTED

73/112

KARATE KUNG-FU!

The oriental sensation – now gives America the action its been waiting for!

every limb of his body is a lethal weapon in

"Fists of Fury"

National General Pictures presents Bruce Lee in "FISTS OF FURY" • Produced by Raymond Chow
Screenplay and Direction by Lo Wei • Color • A National General Pictures Release

73/112

KARATE KUNG-FU!

The oriental sensation – now gives America the action its been waiting for!

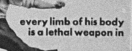

every limb of his body is a lethal weapon in

"Fists of Fury"

National General Pictures presents Bruce Lee in "FISTS OF FURY" • Produced by Raymond Chow
Screenplay and Direction by Lo Wei • Color • A National General Pictures Release

THE BIG BOSS

This is the first of Bruce Lee's kung fu classics. Bruce arrives in Bangkok and goes to work in an ice-making factory. Things are not as they appear. He soon finds himself drawn into a web of evil from which only his integrity and great fighting skills can save him.

Starring: Bruce Lee
Directed by: Lo Wei

STAR SHOP

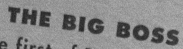

NEW YORK HAS BEEN WAITING FOR AUTHENTIC KARATE KUNG-FU ACTION AND "FISTS OF FURY" DELIVERS THE BIGGEST KICK.

"There's clearly an audience for super hero **Bruce Lee**, his fists and their stomach—collapsing wallop."
—CUE MAGAZINE

"Fists of Fury"

A National General Pictures Release

The film that made **BRUCE LEE...**

THE **BIG BOSS**

...the film that makes the action!

Producer: Raymond Chow.
Distributed by Cathay Films Ltd

DON'T BE FOOLED BY IMITATIONS. "FISTS OF FURY" IS THE ONLY AUTHENTIC KARATE KUNG-FU FILM YOU CAN SEE IN NEW YORK THIS WEEK!

Bruce Lee
The oriental superstar who breaks records the way he breaks heads!

"Fists of Fury"

KARATE KUNG-FU!

The new screen excitement that gives you the biggest kick of your life!

Bruce Lee
"Fists of Fury"

POSTERS, PICTURES & PRESS BOOKS

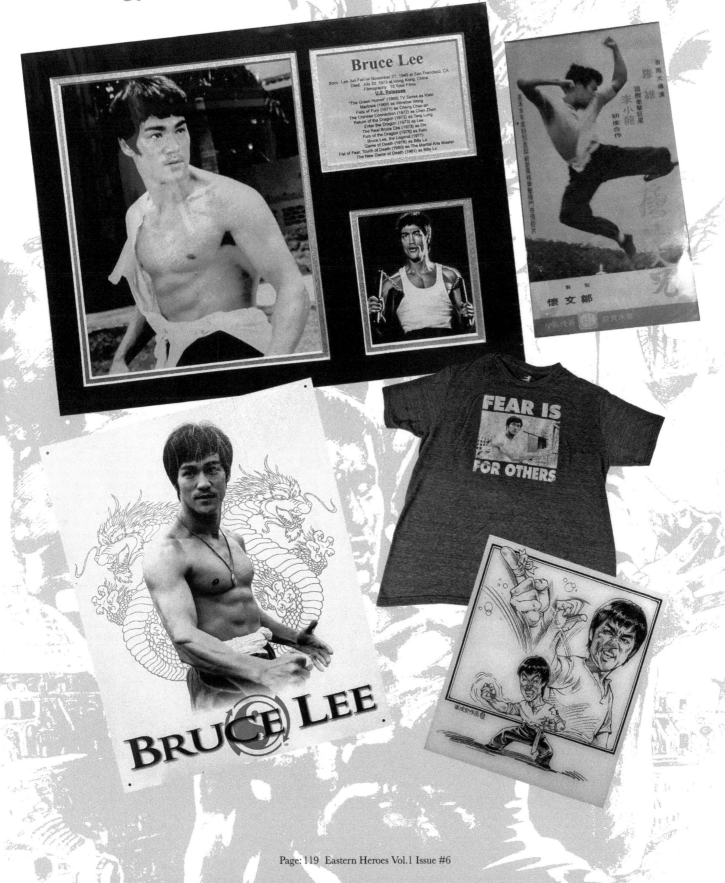

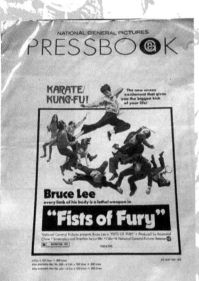

BRUCE | TEA

GINSENG, ROYAL JELLY & HONEY:
BLEND BY BRUCE LEE

"Always be yourself, express yourself, have faith in yourself."

MODELS & FIGURES

ENTER THE DRAGON

PHOTO GALLERY

龍爭虎鬥

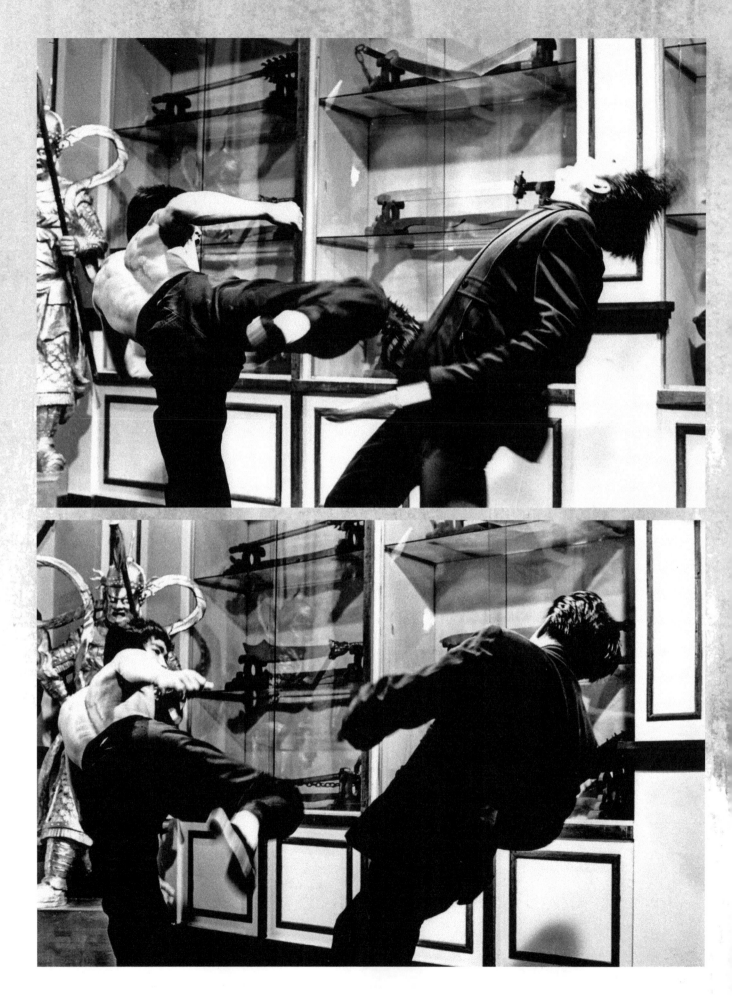

KARATE/
KUNG-FU!

The new screen
excitement that gives
you the biggest kick
of your life!

Bruce Lee
every limb of his body is a lethal weapon in

**THOMAS GROSS
COLLECTION**

National General Pictures presents Bruce Lee in "FISTS OF FURY" • Produced by Raymond Chow • Screenplay and Direction by Lo Wei • Color • A National General Pictures Release

THEATRE

BRUCE LEE

Lobby Cards

BRUCE LEE, THE MASTER OF "KARATE/KUNG FU" in
"FISTS OF FURY"
A National General Pictures Release

BRUCE LEE, THE MASTER OF "KARATE/KUNG FU" in
"FISTS OF FURY"
A National General Pictures Release

BRUCE LEE, THE MASTER OF "KARATE/KUNG FU" in
"FISTS OF FURY"
A National General Pictures Release   Color

5   73/112

BRUCE LEE, THE MASTER OF "KARATE/KUNG FU" in
"FISTS OF FURY"
A National General Pictures Release   Color   73/112

BRUCE LEE, THE MASTER OF "KARATE/KUNG FU" in
"FISTS OF FURY"
A National General Pictures Release   Color

7   COPYRIGHT ©1973 NATIONAL GENERAL PICTURES CORP.   LITHO. IN U.S.A.   73/112

BRUCE LEE, THE MASTER OF "KARATE/KUNG FU" in
"FISTS OF FURY"
A National General Pictures Release   Color   73/112

DIE TODESFAUST DES **CHENG LI**

DIE TODESFAUST DES **CHENG LI**

DIE TODESFAUST DES **CHENG LI**

DIE TODESFAUST DES **CHENG LI**

DIE TODESFAUST DES **CHENG LI**

DIE TODESFAUST DES **CHENG LI**

DIE TODESFAUST DES **CHENG LI**

DIE TODESFAUST DES **CHENG LI**

DIE TODESFAUST DES **CHENG LI**

DIE TODESFAUST DES **CHENG LI**

DIE TODESFAUST DES **CHENG LI**

DIE TODESFAUST DES **CHENG LI**

DIE TODESFAUST DES **CHENG LI**

DIE TODESFAUST DES **CHENG LI**

DIE TODESFAUST DES **CHENG LI**

兄大山唐
THE BIG BOSS

兄大山唐
THE BIG BOSS

兄大山唐
THE BIG BOSS

兄大山唐
THE BIG BOSS

兄大山唐
THE BIG BOSS

兄大山唐
THE BIG BOSS

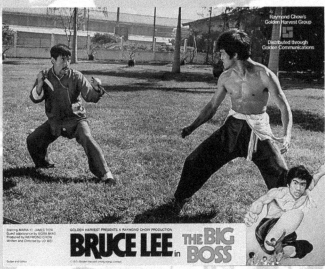

Starring MARIA YI JAMES TIEN
Guest appearance by NORA MIAO
Produced by RAYMOND CHOW
Written and Directed by LO WEI

Raymond Chow's
Golden Harvest Group

Distributed through
Golden Communications

GOLDEN HARVEST PRESENTS A RAYMOND CHOW PRODUCTION

BRUCE LEE in **THE BIG BOSS**

Scope and Colour   ©1971 Golden Harvest (Hong Kong) Limited

Starring MARIA YI JAMES TIEN
Guest appearance by NORA MIAO
Produced by RAYMOND CHOW
Written and Directed by LO WEI

Raymond Chow's
Golden Harvest Group

Distributed through
Golden Communications

GOLDEN HARVEST PRESENTS A RAYMOND CHOW PRODUCTION

BRUCE LEE in **THE BIG BOSS**

Scope and Colour   ©1971 Golden Harvest (Hong Kong) Limited

EIN ECHTER BRUCE LEE

DIE TODESFAUST DES CHENG Li

DIE TODESFAUST DES CHENG Li

DIE TODESFAUST DES CHENG Li

DIE TODESFAUST DES CHENG Li

DIE TODESFAUST DES CHENG Li

DIE TODESFAUST DES CHENG Li

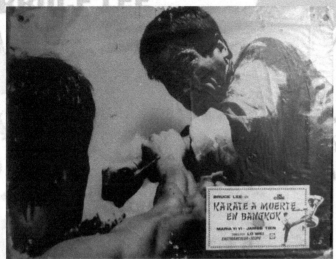

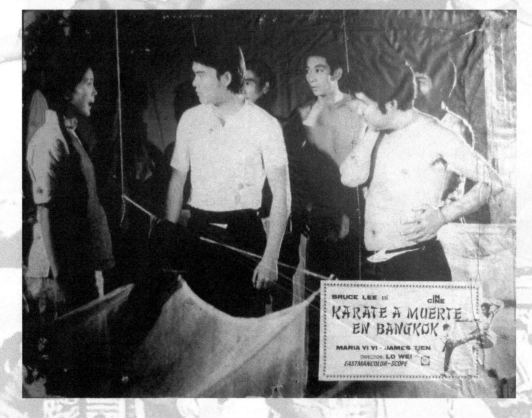

ANDRE GENOVES présente

Big Boss

COULEURS

Une distribution LES FILMS LA BOETIE
diffusée par CINEMA INTERNATIONAL CORPORATION

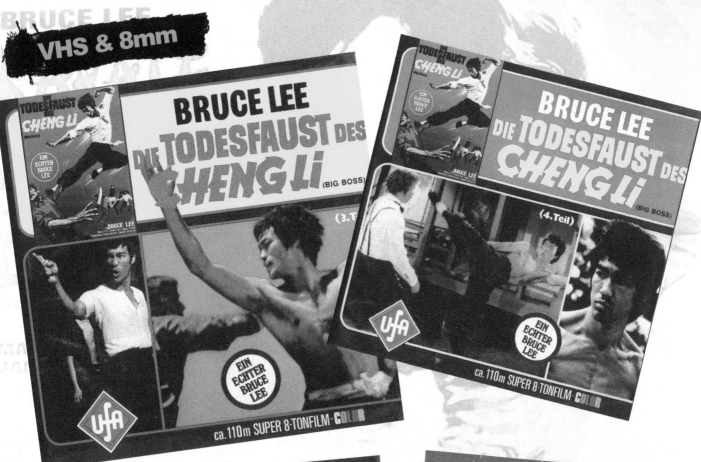

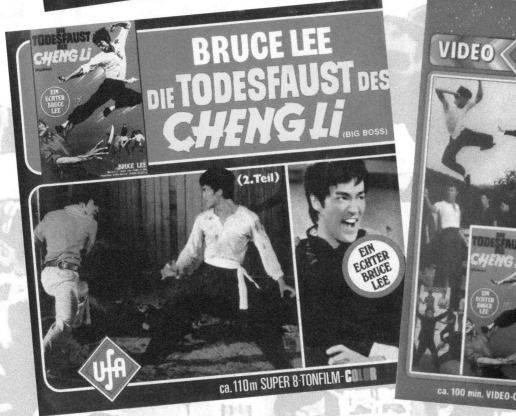

THE BIG BOSS

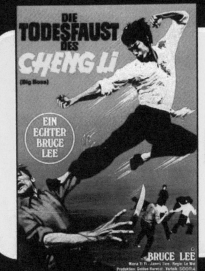

Posters

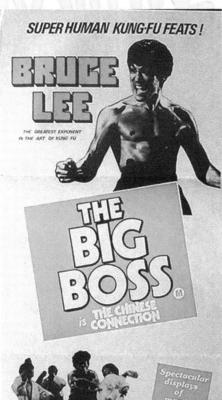

SUPER HUMAN KUNG-FU FEATS !

BRUCE LEE

THE GREATEST EXPONENT IN THE ART OF KUNG-FU

THE BIG BOSS is THE CHINESE CONNECTION

Spectacular displays of martial arts that will leave you breathless!

unstoppable
unbelievable
unbeatable

"THE CHINESE CONNECTION"

COLOR

BRUCE LEE

REGRESA EL INMORTAL DRAGON!

Circuito presidente ltda
20 años

BRUCE LEE

Golden Harvest Group

Distributed through Golden Communications

video presidente

PPeliculas presidente

EL GRAN JEFE

CIRCUITO PRESIDENTE LTDA 1.988

أفلام مصر العربية تقدم

الرأس الكبير بروس لي

BRUCE LEE in THE BIG BOSS

BRUCE LEE
REY DEL KUNG FU

CON JAMES TIEN • MARIA YI
Dirección LO WEY

BRUCE LEE

unstoppable!
unbelievable!
unbeatable!

the master of kung fu
will break you up,
smash you down and kick you apart with

"THE CHINESE CONNECTION"

WATCH FOR IT AT THE STATE SOON

COLOR

Italian first print poster

French Poster: 1973

EASTERN-HELTEN
NR.1
BRUCE
LEE

ENSPLOSIONSAGTIGE
KARATE-SLAGSMÅL

KARATE-NÆVER
AF STÅL

FARVER OG SCOPE

Denmark first release

Får alle tidligere action-film
til at ligne sypige-historier

Denmark rare release

No evil on earth could survive the fury that was Bruce Lee!

GOLDEN HARVEST PRESENTS A RAYMOND CHOW PRODUCTION

BRUCE LEE in THE BIG BOSS

Greek poster

German poster

Singapore poster

Italian posetr

Titanus

BRUCE LEE

IL FURORE DELLA CINA COLPISCE ANCORA

PRODOTTO DA **LO WEI**   REGIA DI **RAYMOND CHOW**   COLORI *Liv* DI **LUCIANO VITTORI**

Italian posetr

USA MondoCon: Texas

KARATE/ KUNG-FU!

The new screen excitement that gives you the biggest kick of your life!

Bruce Lee

every limb of his body is a lethal weapon in

"Fists of Fury"

National General Pictures presents Bruce Lee in "FISTS OF FURY" • Produced by Raymond Chow
Screenplay and Direction by Lo Wei • Color • A National General Pictures Release

USA poster

"FISTS OF FURY"

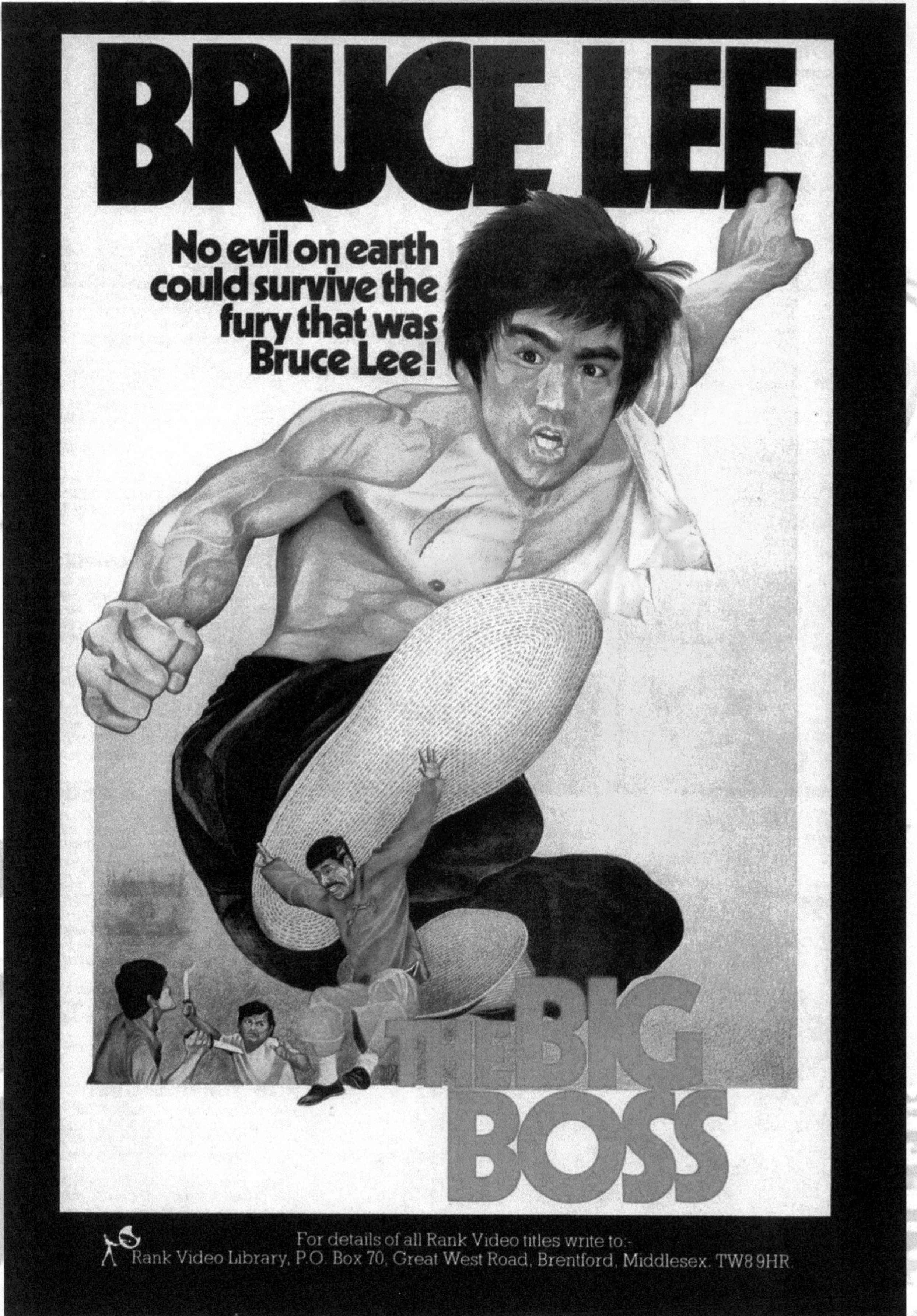

UK Video advert

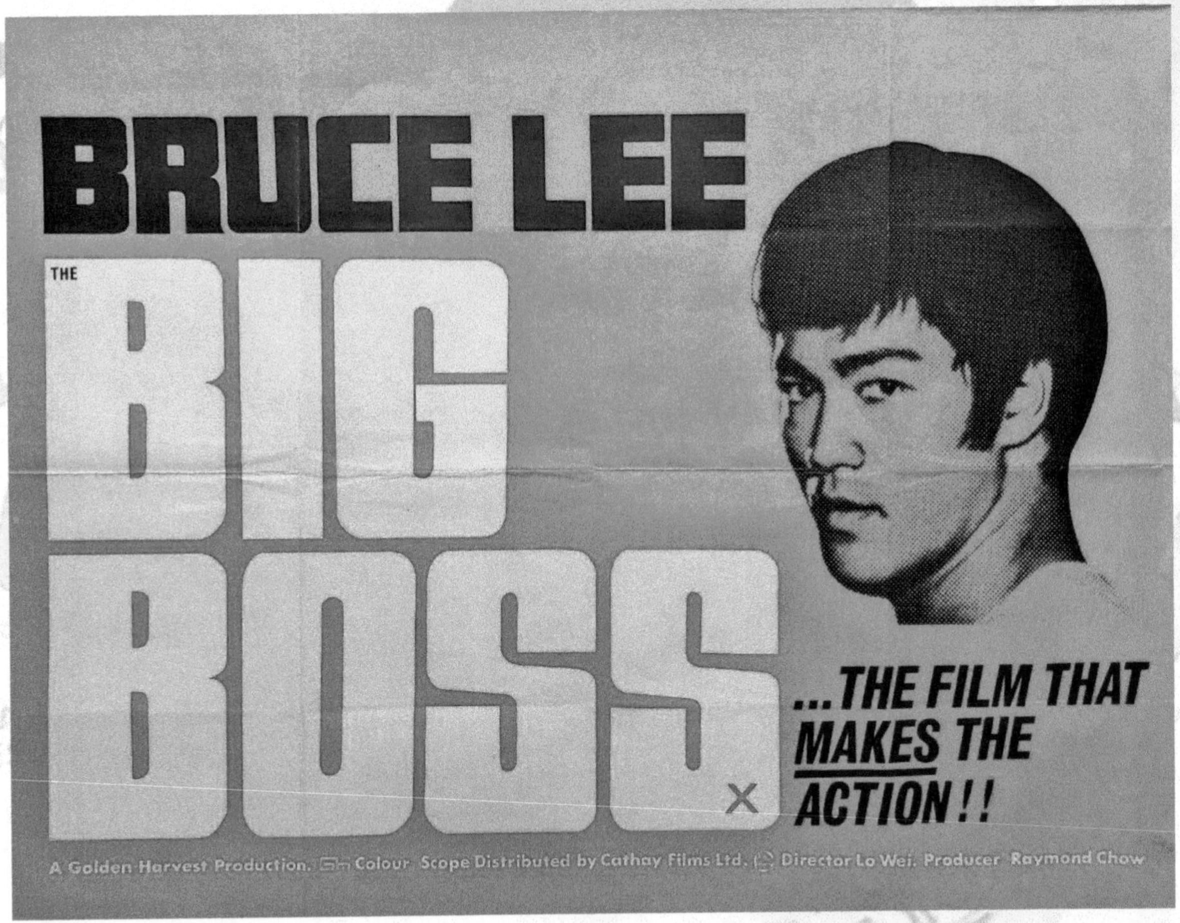

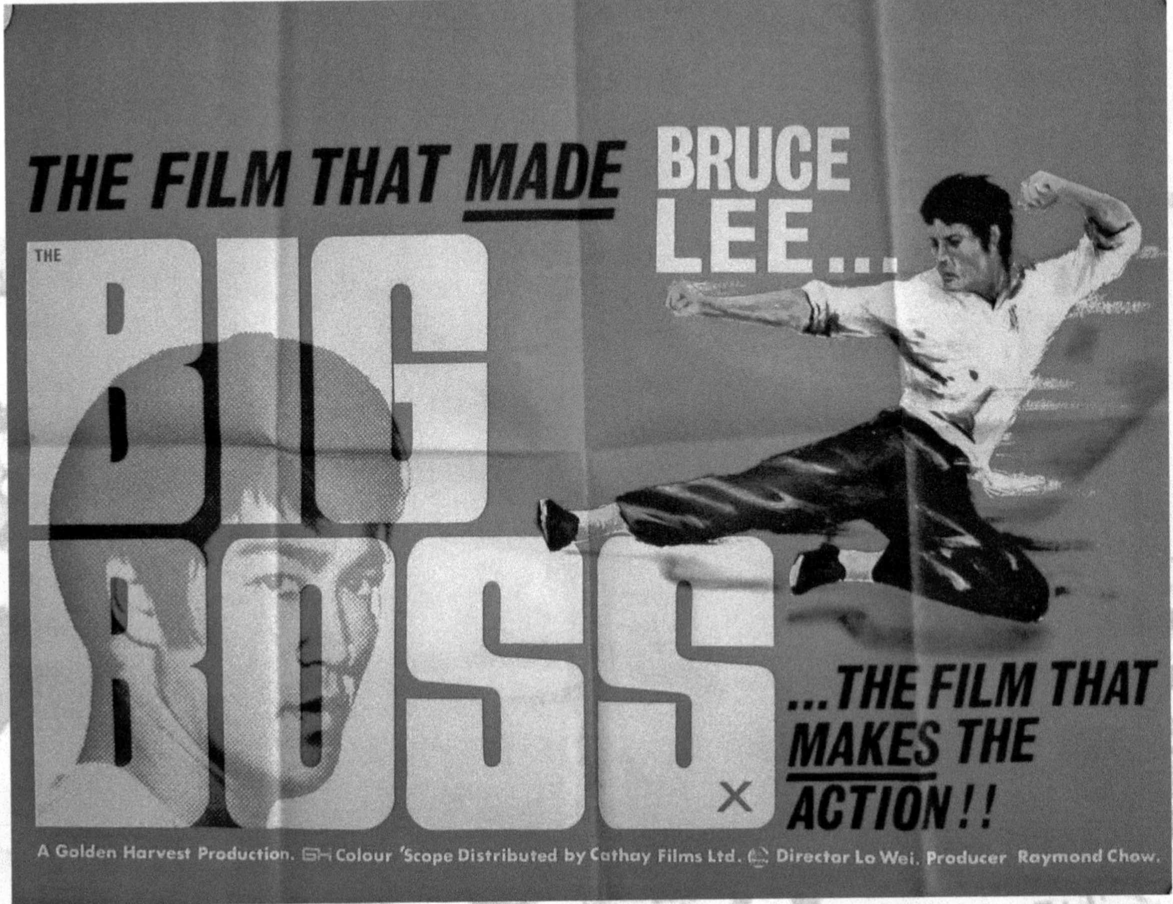

UK quad poster variants

ΚΑΙ ΤΩΡΑ... Ο ΘΡΥΛΟΣ ΤΩΝ ΘΡΥΛΩΝ
ΣΤΗΝ ΠΙΟ ΜΕΓΑΛΗ, ΤΗΝ ΠΙΟ ΕΝΤΥΠΩΣΙΑΚΗ ΕΜΦΑΝΙΣΗ ΤΟΥ

ΜΠΡΟΥΣ ΛΗ

ΔΡΑΣΗ ΠΟΥ ΔΕΝ ΣΤΑΜΑΤΑΕΙ ΛΕΠΤΟ...
ΠΕΡΙΠΕΤΕΙΑ ΜΕ ΠΡΩΤΟΓΝΩΡΑ ΚΟΛΠΑ...

ΞΑΝΑΖΕΙΣΤΕ ΣΤΙΓΜΕΣ
ΠΟΥ ΜΟΝΟ Ο
ΜΠΡΟΥΣ ΛΗ
ΞΕΡΕΙ ΝΑ ΧΑΡΙΖΕΙ...

Ο ΜΕΓΑΛΟΣ ΑΡΧΗΓΟΣ
(THE BIG BOSS)

Συμπρωταγωνιστούν : ΜΑΙΡΗ ΓΕΗΤΣ - ΤΖΕΗΜΣ ΤΗΝ
Διανομή: ΝΕΑ ΚΙΝΗΣΗ Α.Ε.Β.Ε.

Greek Poster

ACKNOWLEDGEMENT

「唐山大兄」本事

「THE BIG BOSS」(synopsis)

THE STORY

THE "FRIENDS OF SCOUTING"

(Affiliate to THE SCOUT ASSOCIATION HONG KONG BRANCH)

Special Performance 3rd November, 1971

PROGRAMME

Audience in Seats

Arrival of H.E. The Commander British Forces,
Lt. General Sir Richard Ward, K.C.B. D.S.O., M.C.,
Patron of the Community Service Organisation

Association Acknowledgement

"THE BIG BOSS"

放影名片（唐山大兄）

放影鳴謝啓事

爵士社會服務隊贊助人臨篤

駐港三軍司令陸軍中將韋道

觀眾就座

義映禮程序表

社會服務籌募運動

義映晚會于一九七一年十一月三日舉行

（香港童軍總會直屬機構）

「**童軍知友**」社

◀◀「唐山大兄」▶▶

演員表

監　製	鄒文懷		導　演	羅　維
鄭　潮安	李小龍		烏　曼	馬拉鏵
巧　梅	衣　依		廠　長	陳　著
許　劍	田　俊		阿　華	陳會毅
阿　昆	李　昆		阿　陰	林正英
沙　密	韓英傑		三　叔	杜家楨
沙　子	劉　承		阿　昌	植耀昌
阿　三	金　山		捱担女	苗可秀(客串)

1971 Hong Kong Premiere Program

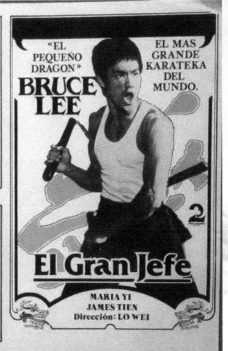

Mexico Newspaper Advert

Pressbook: Germany

Greek advert

History's Most Successful Chinese Picture:
THE BIG BOSS

"THE BIG BOSS" tells its story in a straight forward but refreshingly forceful manner. It is frank about sex and violence.

Young Bruce Lee from back country comes to town for work. He finds it, plus many friends and love.

He also meets Evil. Narcotic smugglers try to pamper him with money and women. Or he is to die like some of his friends did.

Bruce does not give in. He has to fight off one villain after another until he finally challenges the arch villain to a fight-till-death.

About the film: In colour and Dyaliscope in 10 reels totaling 9284 feet.

Running time: 103 minutes.

Director: Lo Wei

Stars: Bruce Lee, Maria Yi,

Producer: Raymond Chow

The Producers:
GOLDEN HARVEST

A group of young, ambitious movie-makers formed Golden Harvest (HK) Limited in May, 1970.

Now, 20 months and 15 films later, these Golden Harvest people have everything a good picture requires: A fresh and sanguine outlook. Complete self-sufficiency in equipment and technology with their own 3-stage studio and colour laboratory. Good planners, directors, writers and actors. Youth backed up by experience and eagerness to experiment. Golden Harvest believes in quality, notably the Chinese quality. Golden Harvest does not preach but lets action tell the story. Golden Harvest is proud to have brought masculinity back to the Chinese screen.

To establish contact, write:

Mr. Raymond Chow President

Golden Harvest (HK) Ltd. 1412, Tung Ying Building 100 Nathan Road Kowloon Tel: K-672144 (4 lines)

Golden Studios 8 Hammersmith Road Kowloon Hong Kong Tel: K-302221 (3 lines) Cable address: "GOLDENSUN" Hongkong

History's Most Successful Chinese Picture:
THE BIG BOSS

"THE BIG BOSS" tells its story in a straight forward but refreshingly forceful manner. It is frank about sex and violence.

Young Bruce Lee from back country comes to town for work. He finds it, plus many friends and love.

He also meets Evil. Narcotic smugglers try to pamper him with money and women. Or he is to die like some of his friends did.

Bruce does not give in. He has to fight off one villain after another until he finally challenges the arch villain to a fight-till-death.

About the film: In colour and Dyaliscope in 10 reels totaling 9284 feet.

Running time: 103 minutes.

Director: Lo Wei

Stars: Bruce Lee, Maria Yi,

Producer: Raymond Chow

The Producers:
GOLDEN HARVEST

A group of young, ambitious movie-makers formed Golden Harvest (HK) Limited in May, 1970.

Now, 20 months and 15 films later, these Golden Harvest people have everything a good picture requires: A fresh and sanguine outlook. Complete self-sufficiency in equipment and technology with their own 3-stage studio and colour laboratory. Good planners, directors, writers and actors. Youth backed up by experience and eagerness to experiment. Golden Harvest believes in quality, notably the Chinese quality. Golden Harvest does not preach but lets action tell the story. Golden Harvest is proud to have brought masculinity back to the Chinese screen.

To establish contact, write:

Mr. Raymond Chow President

Golden Harvest (HK) Ltd. 1412, Tung Ying Building 100 Nathan Road Kowloon Tel: K-672144 (4 lines)

Golden Studios 8 Hammersmith Road Kowloon Hong Kong Tel: K-302221 (3 lines) Cable address: "GOLDENSUN" Hongkong

BRUCE LEE

"Little Dragon" Bruce is the idol of Chinese moviegoers. He is one actor who always seeks improvement.

Young as he is, Bruce was the acknowledged teacher-master in the United States of Jeet-Kuen-Do, a form of Chinese martial art.

Disarmingly frank and friendly, Bruce is deadly serious in work.

His next picture is "FIST OF FURY"

WANG YU

Wang Yu is versatility itself — an expert in fencing, karate, boxing both the Western and Chinese styles, car racing. He directs, acts and writes the script.

Himself, a box office record holder, he is the trailblazer in Chinese action films.

His next picture is "ONE-ARMED BOXER"

Announcing:
The Invasion of the
CHINESE BLOCK-BUSTER!

"THE BIG BOSS" in English.

"THE BIG BOSS" is Chinese, very Chinese. It tells of Chinese restraint and self-discipline. But when fight he must, the Chinese fights to win.

"THE BIG BOSS" is action, thrilling action. It also presents the kind of tender love only Chinese are capable of.

"THE BIG BOSS" thinks clean, fights dirty.

"THE BIG BOSS" is the prize product of Golden Harvest, foremost Chinese producers based in Hong Kong.

"THE BIG BOSS" holds the all time box office record of Hong Kong and Singapore, the only places in Asia that it has been released so far. It now has English and Chinese dialogue versions.

Two other Golden Harvest pictures of international fame:

"Zatoichi & One-Armed Swordsman"

"The Fast Sword"

Starring: Wang Yu, Shintaro Katsu

Starring: Chang Yi

BRUCE LEE

"Little Dragon" Bruce is the idol of Chinese moviegoers. He is one actor who always seeks improvement.

Young as he is, Bruce was the acknowledged teacher-master in the United States of Jeet-Kuen-Do, a form of Chinese martial art.

Disarmingly frank and friendly, Bruce is deadly serious in work.

His next picture is "FIST OF FURY"

WANG YU

Wang Yu is versatility itself — an expert in fencing, karate, boxing both the Western and Chinese styles, car racing. He directs, acts and writes the script.

Himself, a box office record holder, he is the trailblazer in Chinese action films.

His next picture is "ONE-ARMED BOXER"

Two other Golden Harvest pictures of international fame:

"Zatoichi & One-Armed Swordsman"

"The Fast Sword"

Starring: Wang Yu, Shintaro Katsu

Starring: Chang Yi

International Promotional Booklet: 1973

Advert: First screening at Cannes 1972

SCOTIA INTERNATIONAL FILMVERLEIH GMBH
DEUTSCHLAND

German pressbook

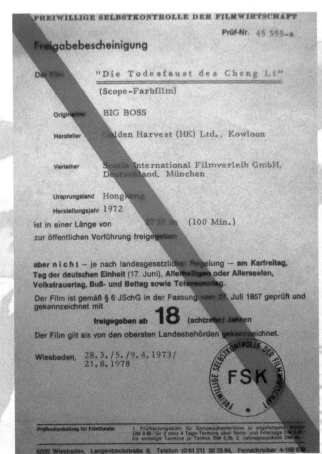

German distributor screening license: 1978

German advertising poster: 1973

Golden Harvest photographs: 1981

Hong Kong Promotional material

Netherlands Movie magazine: 1973

Korean advert

Greek press photographs

Japanese press photo set

NATIONAL GENERAL PICTURES

PRESSBOOK

KARATE/ KUNG-FU!

The new screen excitement that gives you the biggest kick of your life!

Bruce Lee
every limb of his body is a lethal weapon in

"Fists of Fury"

National General Pictures presents Bruce Lee in "FISTS OF FURY" • Produced by Raymond Chow • Screenplay and Direction by Lo Wei • Color • A National General Pictures Release

R RESTRICTED

THEATRE

4 Col. x 125 Lines = 500 Lines
Also available Mat No. 302—3 Col. x 100 Lines = 300 Lines
Also available Mat No. 401—4 Col. x 125 Lines = 500 Lines

AD MAT NO. 402

Press book USA: 1973

Hong Kong promotional poster

Australian press sheet

Singapore flyer

Thailand promotional poster

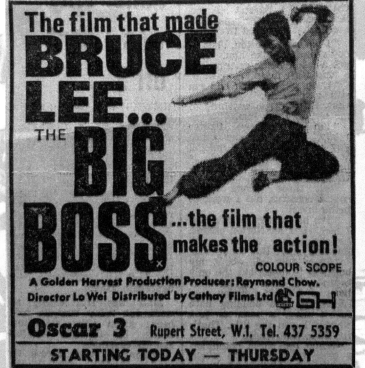

UK newspaper adverts

BRUCE LEE THE WAY OF THE DRAGON

Presented and hand-painted by Siew Lam Chong
The first ever highly detailed hand painted comic in the world.
Made frame by frame, from Bruce Lee's 1972 film

"Way of the Dragon"
Capturing Bruce, with his many facial expressions, and lightning speed often too quick for the camera to capture without doubt the most realistic- drawn Bruce Lee comic you have ever seen.

Last year I showcased in several issues of my Bruce Lee special magazines the amazing and stunning art work of Siew Lam Chong.

And I am excited to say that after a year of his dedication, the book which had so many people were talking about and messaging me is finally ready for you to enjoy.
His artwork and attention to detail is breath-taking and this will surely be something that any Bruce Lee fan will want to own.

I truly hope that he is inspired to reproduce other Bruce Lee Movies in the same colourful and fantastic detail that we see here.

Do not hesitate to grab a copy now available both in "Special hardcover Edition" printed with high quality premium ink and there is also a paperback version available too.

Truly a masterpiece of visual viewing for any Bruce lee fan
Rick Baker

FANATICAL FD DRAGON PRESENTS

5 FINGERS OF DISCS

Greetings once again dear friends, in tribute to Darren Wheeling,
our guest cover artist this issue this time around I'm helping
to showcase a few of the wealth of covers he's created for some
exceptional Eureka Blu-ray releases, past, present and future.
Let's dive right in with the Cop who can't be stopped…

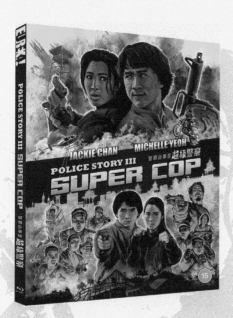

1) Police Story III - Supercop
Eureka Entertainment
Region B Blu-ray
Available now.

Last issue I looked at Eureka's absolutely fantastic 4K boxset of Jackie Chan's three best Police Story movies, but also released at the same time was this outstanding standalone regular Blu-ray release of PS3 with all the same great extra features found on the 4K disc but with the added inclusion of 4 reproduction lobby cards, which a very welcome addition. There are two main pieces of artwork created by Darren for the release, one for the limited edition slipcase and one on the reversible inner sleeve. This is truly an ideal companion to Eureka's previous Police Story 1+2 release
(or the stunning US Criterion boxset of parts 1+2) Just like on the 4K set, the extra features on the set are extensive and extremely well produced. Both the two newly created commentary tracks (one by Frank Djeng and Fj Desanto and the other by Big Mike Leeder and Arne Venema) are first rate, offering up a great mix of facts, memories from the hosts and lots of laughs.
Arne Venema's two video extras, a HK location guide to the PS trilogy and a dive into the various Jackie Chan computer games created over the years are both absolutely fantastic. Hours of archival interviews, outtakes and trailers round out a truly spectacular release. The regular blu-ray holds up surprisingly well against the 4K UHD disc, there is obviously more detail and definition on display on the 4K release, but this regular Blu-Ray still looks

absolutely fantastic. The included lobby card reproductions are a really nice touch too, something I personally wish Eureka will do more of in their releases moving forward. They help to really round out what is one of the best standalone releases of 2022.

2) Angela Mao Double Pack - Lady Whirlwind / Hapkido
Eureka Entertainment
Region B Blu-Ray
Available now.

Bringing together two of our previous Cover Star Angela Mao's most beloved titles into one glorious special edition double pack. Featuring all new 2K restorations of Huang Feng's Lady Whirlwind and the exceptional Hapkido. Last month saw Eureka release their side of another in their ongoing collaborations with Arrow Video. Eureka have released the two movies here in the UK in a special edition with Darren's Artwork on the slipcase, menu screens and booklet. Arrow Video will release the same disc with their own artwork in the USA later in January 2023. The UK edition showcased here comes along with a great reversible poster featuring the alternate titles and original International posters for the two movies. This is also the title that includes the wonderful interview footage Frank Djeng shot with Angela in NY that he recorded at the same time as the interview which graced the pages of the Angela Mao Eastern Heroes issue. In addition to that great video there is also a stack of dedicated commentary tracks for each movie, three tracks for Lady Whirlwind, two from Frank Djeng, one where he's

joined by another great Eastern Heroes collaborator Michael Worth and a second track where he's joined by Robert 'Bobby' Samuels along with a third track from film journalist and author Samm Deighan. We also get an interview with Angela Mao's son Thomas King, alternate English Credits, a stills gallery and a radio spot for the 1972 classic.

Hapkido is presented in another glorious brand new 2k restoration, the movie looks absolutely jaw dropping. Light years ahead of the old Hong Kong Legends DVD which I saw the movie on last. Extras wise we get two more highly entertaining Frank Djeng commentary tracks, again joined by Michael Worth for one and by Robert Samuels for the other. more of Frank's all new interview with Angela Mao and also the old archival interviews from the Hong Kong Legends DVD with Co-stars Carter Wong and Sammo Hung and of course with Lady Kung Fu herself, Angela Mao. All round its one of the best double sets Eureka have put out so far and showcases one of Darren's most striking pieces so far on the cover.

Highly, highly recommended.

3) The Dead and The Deadly
Eureka Entertainment
Region B - Bluray
21st November 2022

Making for a great companion to Sammo Hung's wonderful Spooky Encounters. In November Eureka will release Wu Ma's 1982 Horror / Action mashup The Dead and the Deadly also starring Sammo Hung alongside the Director himself

Wu Ma joined by Lam Ching-Ying and Cherie Chung. Darren's cover art for the title shares a fairly similar colour palette to his previous work on Spooky Encounters and this release looks no less loaded with extras.

Once again Frank Djeng is joined by Michael Worth on commentary duties and we again get a second track by the HK dynamic Duo of Big Mike Leeder and Arne Venema.

Frederic Ambroisine also makes a very welcome contribution to the disc with the inclusion of some of his archival gold, in this instance video recorded of Sammo Hung at the 2016 Udine Far East Film Festival. A limited edition booklet is also planned with writing once again by James Oliver. For those not familiar with this movie, Wu Ma stars as a man who fakes his death in order to steal his family's funeral treasure. When the treasure is instead bequeathed to Ma's unborn son, his co-conspirators kill him (for real this time). His vengeful spirit seeks out the help of his friend (played by Sammo Hung) and together they seek revenge on his murderers. It would of been nice if this arrived in time for Halloween, but that's a moot point as the release will be

entertaining us for many years to come. It's great to see a less well known Wu Ma movie getting the Royal treatment it so richly deserves!

4) Yes Madam / Royal Warriors
Eureka Entertainment
Region B - Bluray
Yes Madame - 12th December 2022
Royal Warriors - 23rd January 2023

Speaking of Royalty, the truly wonderful Royal Warriors (and the even more wonderful Yes Madam) are both incoming and their arrival also ushering in another round of battle in the ongoing Blu-ray wars between the various Boutique Labels offering up competing editions of the same movies on different sides of the Atlantic.

Eureka will begin their focus on the In the Line of Duty Movies with the first two instalments of the series, Yes Madam and Royal Warriors being released in December and January respectively. I'd be remiss however, if I didn't mention that 88 Films will ALSO be releasing the first four movies grouped together in one single

boxset in the US early next year.

In the UK, Eureka will be putting out the movies initially with the two individual titles mentioned here along with a double feature of In the Line of Duty 3 and 4 to follow later in the year. There is talk of a specially created rigid box to house the releases also coming from the label, but no definite word on that at the time of going to print.

What we do know so far is that Darren

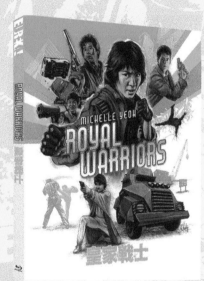

- NEW 2K RESTORATION
- THEATRICAL AND EXPORT CUTS OF THE FILM
- CANTONESE MONO & ENGLISH DUBBED AUDIO
- NEWLY TRANSLATED OPTIONAL ENGLISH SUBTITLES
- NEW AUDIO COMMENTARY TRACKS
- SELECT-SCENE COMMENTARY WITH CYNTHIA ROTHROCK

- NEW CYNTRHIA ROTHROCK INTERVIEW
- NEW MANG HOI INTERVIEW
- ARCHIVAL MICHELLE YEOH INTERVIEW
- BATTLING BABES FEATURETTE
- LOCATIONS FEATURETTE
- TRAILERS

RELEASE DATE:
12/12/2022

will once again be creating the Eureka titles artwork for the movies and that the extras for Yes Madam and Royal Warriors look fantastic. Along with a Brand new 2K restoration of each movie Eureka have provided brand new audio commentaries by Frank Djeng & Michael Worth along with a second track for each film by Mike and Arne. A select scene commentary from Cynthia Rothrock is also planned for Yes Madam. On the video extras side we get a locations featurette as well as archival interviews with Michelle Yeah and John Shum, Original trailers and a reversible sleeve round out the on disc extras for each movie. The first 2000 copies of each release will also get one of Eureka's great booklets with writings from James Oliver. More details are still to be announced for Royal Warriors.

5) **And the other best of the rest from Eureka.....**
   Cinematic Vengeance Boxset
   Warriors Two / The Prodigal Son
   The Odd Couple
   The Shaolin Plot
   Duel to the Death
   Dreadnaught
   Knockabout
   Encounters of the Spooky Kind
   Mr Vampire
   Millionaires Express

   All from Eureka Entertainment
   All titles are Region B

In previous issues of Eastern Heroes (most notably in the Sammo Hung special) I've covered numerous Eureka titles which all feature Darren's work on their limited edition slipcovers and inner sleeves. All the titles above I can't say enough good things about, Please refer back to earlier issues for more specific details on the other titles in Eureka's Martial Arts series of releases, but rest assured all of these have been gloriously remastered to look their very best and all come loaded with very similar extras to those mentioned on the other titles this issue.

It's truly great to have another UK label so dedicated to bringing out high quality, well realised special editions of the movies a great many of us fell in love with decades ago and the films that a whole new generation are getting to experience for the very first time!
Truth be told, I'm rather jealous of them

for getting to experience them in such high quality for their first time viewings!

Long may this new Golden Age of HK Physical Media reign!

For movie reviews, upcoming Blu-ray release information and unboxing videos and to also be able to chat with other Kung Fu and Martial Arts Blu-ray collectors,
take a minute to jump on over and find me on Youtube, where I post regular updates and new videos every few days.

Written by Johnny 'The Fanatical Dragon' Burnett

www.youtube.com/thefanaticaldragon

THANK YOU'S

Compiled by Rick Baker
Cover Design & Interior layout
Tim Hollingsworth
Darren Wheeling (USA)
Mike Nesbitt (UK)
Simon Pritchard (UK)
Alan Donkin (UK)
Alan Canvan (USA)
Jason McNeil (USA)
John Negron (USA)
Demetrius Angelo (USA)

Special Thanks to
John Negron for his memorabilia
Thomas Gross for memorabilia

OTHER BRUCE LEE EDITIONS AVAILABLE

CPSIA information can be obtained
at www.ICGtesting.com
Printed in the USA
BVHW012154100323
660241BV00002B/28